Smart Skills: Negotiation

Anthony Jacks worked in sales, sales management and marketing before joining a management institute and then moving into consultancy and training. He was a director of a medium-sized consultancy before setting up his own operation. He now has more than twenty-five years of experience as a successful trainer, working in a wide variety of industries, in overseas markets as well as the United Kingdom. He specialises in developing communications skills such as selling, negotiation, business writing and making presentations. He has also written on a variety of business matters and is the author of *How to Be Better at Marketing* (Kogan Page).

Other books in the Smart Skills series

Meetings
Mastering the Numbers
Persuasion
Presentations
Working With Others

www.smartskillsbooks.com

Smart Skills: Negotiation

Anthony Jacks

RUPA

Copyright © Anthony Jacks 2011

First published in India in 2012 by
Rupa Publications India Pvt. Ltd.
7/16, Ansari Road, Daryaganj
New Delhi 110 002

Sales Centres:

Allahabad Bengaluru Chennai
Hyderabad Jaipur Kathmandu
Kolkata Mumbai

First published in 2011 by Legend Business, London, UK.

This edition published by arrangement
with the original publisher.

All rights reserved.
No part of this publication may be reproduced, stored in a retrieval system, or transmitted, in any form or by any means, electronic, mechanical, photocopying, recording or otherwise, without the prior permission of the publishers.

10 9 8 7 6 5 4 3 2 1

Anthony Jacks asserts the moral right to be
identified as the author of this work.

This edition is for sale in India only.

CONTENTS

FOREWORD by Jonathan Reuvid	7
INTRODUCTION: **Getting the best deal**	9
1. NEGOTIATION: **Getting to grips with the core approaches**	24
2. PREPARATION: **The route to achieving success**	30
3. TRADING: **Achieving successful balance**	43
4. MAKING IT WORK: **Good tactics, bad tactics and downright ploys**	51
5. THE INTERPERSONAL DIMENSION: **The behavioural interactions**	68
6. THE FINE PRINT: **The contractual elements of a deal**	86
7. FOCUSING ON THE KEY ISSUES: **Attention to detail**	98
Glossary of terms	112

Foreword

Myriads of management handbooks in print purport to provide guidance on the key skills to success and business training manuals also abound. Generally, they suffer from one or both of two defects.

Sometimes, the scope of the book is too broad. Attempting to provide comprehensive advice on all the basic business activities, there is no clear message. Nobody can gain proficiency in every field of marketing and sales, administration, purchasing, bookkeeping and financial management in a short period of time, although those who start their own businesses do need to acquire a working knowledge of most. Other titles fail to distinguish between technical capability and personal skills.

However, there are a handful of personal and interpersonal skills that are essential ingredients for success in any business: the private or public sectors and the professions; large or small organisations; employees, business owners or management consultants. These are the subject matter of the Smart Skills series on which all readers can focus to advantage because mastery of them will surely enhance both job satisfaction and their careers.

All the skills that you have acquired in reading other titles in this series are deployed on the playing field of negotiation, whether for new or repeat business, in one deal situations or long-term projects, and in the easy-to-read format of this Anthony Jacks' book, *Negotiation*. Securing the best deal available through the negotiation process is at the heart of all successful business and readers are lead through the preparation work, managing the tight corners during negotiations and the after-negotiation period when what has been agreed needs to be put into effect. From Anthony's practical and painstaking approach to the various steps in negotiation you will be able to acquire your personal skills set as a negotiator.

In the *Smart Skills Series* Anthony and his fellow authors bring together their know-how of core skills into a single compact series. Whatever your level of experience and the rung of your career ladder that you have reached, this book will help you to audit your personal effectiveness and raise your game when interacting with others.

Jonathan Reuvid

INTRODUCTION:
Getting the best deal

'You don't get what you deserve; you get what you negotiate.'
Anon

The saying quoted above strikes a good note on which to begin a review of the process of negotiation. Negotiation – bargaining to put it simply – is a vital skill, one used in very many different contexts in business and organisational life.

Negotiation is essentially the important process of making a deal and agreeing the arrangements on which it is arranged; as such it is a ubiquitous, indeed essential, business skill, and it is worth noting up front that it is both:

- **An interactive communication skill**, one that must be deployed in many different circumstances and at every level of organisational life. It is a close partner of persuasive communication skills, including sales situations. It may also need to be utilised in a wide variety of business dealings from union negotiation to corporate takeover and merger arrangements as well as a myriad of more everyday situations.
- **A career skill**, in the sense that it is one of those skills – along with a number of others including being able to present formally, write a good report and manage your time – that many (perhaps most) people working in an organisation need. These skills are necessary not only to deploy in doing a job successfully, but are needed if someone is to be seen as fully competent. And excelling

in such areas enhances the likelihood of career success. Negotiation may also be needed to obtain the best deal – and remuneration package – for yourself.

Good negotiators are in a strong position to make a good impression and a good deal.

A MEANS TO AN END

A great deal can be riding on the outcome of a negotiation. Success in negotiating can make money, save time or secure your future (and your reputation). To negotiate and do so successfully is to deploy a technique that can work positively for you in a host of different ways. The overall deal you strike may be vital, and individual elements of it can be significant, perhaps very significant. For example, without a little negotiation regarding the delivery date for the manuscript for this work, I could not have taken it on and would have missed the opportunity that writing it provides for me.

The uses of negotiation

Negotiation has a variety of applications. The following illustrates the range:

- As part of the sales process (by both buyer and seller).
- Between individuals for primarily personal reasons (e.g. negotiating a pay increase or remuneration package, or "discussing" with your boss when to can take your holiday).
- In wage bargaining (as between an employer organisation and a union or staff group).
- In political circles (as in treaties between governments).
- Internationally (either between individuals or organisations in different countries or literally on a worldwide basis – like the talks about measures to combat global warming).
- In corporate affairs (takeovers, mergers and a variety of alliances and collaborations, sought or forced by circumstances).

Negotiation often involves a financial element (though it may not) and can involve two people or groups of people and take place at every level of an organisational hierarchy. Finally, it may be momentary and minor – if you can deputise for me at tomorrow's meeting, I can give you a little longer on that deadline we spoke about – but still needs getting right.

In all cases negotiation is the process of *bargaining* that arranges and agrees the basis on which agreement will be concluded – the terms and conditions under which the deal will be struck. Consider a simple example. In the classic case of wage bargaining, the employer wants to reach an agreement (to secure the workforce and keep the business running) and the employees want an agreement (so that the process of negotiating is over and they can get on with earning at a new, improved, rate). This process of balance defines the process.

In selling, the first stage is to get agreement – from the point of view of the seller *to get what they want* – but beyond that, negotiation is what *decides the "best deal"*. Thus if you are buying a car, say, then the things that need arrangement are all those making up the "package", which goes beyond just the car itself. Such factors may include: the finance, discounts, and extras to be included with the car (air-conditioning, perhaps) that are not standard, or delivery, trade in of an existing vehicle and more.

MAKING IT WORK

The techniques of negotiation are many and varied. It needs the right approach, the right attitude and attention to a multitude of details on the way through. Like so many business skills it cannot be applied by rote; its use must be tailored – intelligently tailored – to the individual circumstances on a case-by-case basis. It has elements of being an adversarial process and it needs handling with care – individual techniques may be common sense in some ways, but they need deploying with some sensitivity. You can as easily find that someone is running rings around you as that you are tying up the deal of a lifetime.

In this book negotiation is explained and investigated. The way it works is spelt out and so doing shows that it is not only important to be able to negotiate, but to be able to plan and manage the process in order to increase the likelihood of achieving the outcome you want.

A changing world

Furthermore it should be said here that negotiation is a frontline skill. It puts those undertaking it in an exposed position. It may involve people within the same organisation or outside it; for instance, much negotiating is traditionally between supplier and buyer. Whatever the precise purpose of negotiation, it is affected by the increasingly dynamic and competitive world in which organisations operate.

For example, buyers negotiating arrangements with suppliers have considerable power and there is always a competitor waiting in the wings to pick up the pieces if a supplier fails to make a deal that is acceptable. Such competitive pressure also exists internally within an organisation and can affect all sorts of negotiation – for instance as people vie for funding for what are in effect competing projects.

However much it may be a skill that needs to be deployed widely within an organisation, and which therefore many people should aim to have as a technique in their armoury, it can certainly also be a high level one. Senior management and leaders of many kinds must be good negotiators.

If the skill of negotiation is one that "goes with the territory" for you, then there is real danger in failing to get to grips with it; and a real opportunity for those who make it their stock in trade.

NEGOTIATION: FIRST PRINCIPLES

Successful negotiation necessitates understanding exactly what negotiation is, why it is a complex process and how exactly it works.

Not all discussions end with a simple yes or no. There will always be many permutations and aspects to be discussed, which have to add up to an outcome acceptable to both, or all, parties. The process of achieving this may take some time. Each aspect has to be considered in turn; and, of course, different people have different ideas about what they want, what is reasonable and how to go about achieving agreement.

So, negotiation is characterised in a number of ways; it is:

- A complex interactive and balanced process and one where the outcome must, by definition, be agreeable to both parties (though that does not mean both parties will necessarily regard the outcome as ideal or exactly equal).

- Adversarial: this element is inherent within the process as each party vies to get the best deal that they can. Keep in mind sayings like that of Ashleigh Brilliant: "I always win. You always lose. What could be fairer than that?" This aspect must be kept in check as if it gets out of hand negotiations may deteriorate into a slanging match with both parties making demands to which neither will ever agree, so that the whole process goes nowhere.
- A process of bargaining and thus of *trading*, in other words as the terms and conditions are discussed – the variables as they are called – must be traded to create a balance on an "if I agree to this, you will need to let me have that" basis.
- A process that involves a fair amount of give and take is necessary, and the to and fro discussion takes time; negotiation cannot be rushed.
- In part a ritual, certainly a ritual element is involved: that is negotiation must be seen to be doing justice to the task it addresses; time is one element of this, as are a variety of procedural matters.

These are all elements that are explored as the book continues, but some thoughts are added here.

Dealing with the adversarial aspect

Returning to the second point above, there is certainly an adversarial aspect to negotiation. To quote another famous remark (something said by Lord Hore-Belisha): "When a man tells me he is going to put all his cards on the table, I always look up his sleeve." Both parties want to win. One of the tricks of successful negotiation, therefore, is for it to end with both sides feeling they have reached a satisfactory conclusion. The adversarial element must be kept in check so that discussions do not deteriorate into a slanging match, with both sides setting impossible conditions and no agreement likely. Only by keeping that aspect under control can it lead to an acceptable outcome for you.

As was said and in part because of this, negotiating involves a fair bit of give and take. You cannot proceed without having an understanding of the other party and their objectives. Ultimately you are after the best deal possible, rather than chasing an unrealistic ideal. None of this happens without the process of to and fro discussion taking on something of a ritualistic element. There are conventions, ways of doing things and unless you keep reasonably close to the fabric of the process, real progress might be jeopardised.

THE ROLE OF NEGOTIATION
Anyone learning and deploying the techniques of negotiation can save themselves or their organisation time and money. Or you may simply put yourself in a stronger position to achieve what you want in discussion.

It is simplistic and obvious to say that negotiation is a form of communication. Yet clearly it must work in communications terms before it can achieve its specific objectives; after all you will not get people to agree to something they do not really understand. So make no mistake: if you do not communicate clearly you will never be a successful negotiator. Furthermore, persuasive communication and negotiation must work together in the right way if the whole communication is to work successfully.

No communication, that is making something clear, is ever easy; think of the regular confusions that you witness, or participate in, around your workplace. Persuasive communication adds an additional dimension and getting someone to do what you want can be downright difficult. Negotiation – agreeing the deal – is something else and the two processes overlap.

- **Communication** is the continuing process, and within that persuasion normally comes first as you have to get the agreement (there is no point in someone bothering about terms, conditions and other arrangements if they do not want something anyway).
- **Negotiation** follows agreement, although negotiation and persuasion can be in train together to some extent, especially in the early stages of a discussion. That said, before we get into the details about negotiation we must set the scene and deal with the basic skills from which it springs.

A SECURE FOUNDATION
Assuredly communication may seem easy. You do it all the time, with

family, friends and day-to-day contacts of all sorts as well as in a business context. Communication may be verbal or in writing. But any communication may have inherent complications. For instance, consider the telephone; this poses problems because you cannot see people and judge their intentions or reactions from facial expressions. Such communication may be emotional, complex or hasty. Consider too the problems that sometimes occur with hastily composed emails. There is always a need for care and to avoid communications breakdown. Whatever form it takes, communication may run into problems because it is:

- Not clear
- Ambiguous and lacking precision
- Incomplete or based on assumptions rather than facts
- Replete with inappropriate jargon.

There are dozens of potential hazards – you may lose the thread of your argument, or the other person may not be listening. Classic examples of communication breakdown abound. One example of simple confusion is the card once used in airports; departing passengers were asked to read it and answer the question: "Has anything been packed in your luggage without your knowledge?" Hmmm: that's a "don't know" then. The late American President, Richard Nixon, is credited with the following convoluted statement: "I know that you think you understand what you think I said, but I am not sure you realise that what you heard is not what I meant." You are certainly going to need to be clearer than that!

This aspect cannot be overstated. If you are clear and communicate with due precision you are more likely to carry others with you. It also contributes to you being seen as professional and a force to be reckoned with – clear communication is the first foundation for successful negotiation.

Leave people unclear about what you mean and you cannot hope to move on to the next stage: of persuading them, which is the precursor to negotiating.

THE POWER TO PERSUADE

This section is an important short digression to examine how you should view the process of being persuasive* and how, by recognising what others are doing in the same circumstances, we can work *with* people to create the mutual agreement that can lead on to a satisfactorily negotiated deal. So what creates a message that acts to persuade and which will relate to the way in which people make decisions to act?

People are often suspicious of someone "with something to sell". Persuasion is synonymous with selling and selling does not always have a very good image. Consider your own reaction to someone trying to sell you double glazing or insurance, particularly when it is done inexpertly or inappropriately; every persuasive message prompts a little of the reaction generated by the worst kind of selling.

The process in view

Your approach must reduce and get over this kind of feeling. How do you do this? Essentially you start by adopting the right attitude to the process. Before you say anything you are going to need to approach it in the right way. Persuading someone must *not* be regarded as a process of "doing something to people". Rather it should be seen as working *with* people; after all any communication inherently involves more than one person. People presented with a possible course of action will want to make up their own minds about it; indeed they will instinctively weigh up the case presented to them and make a considered decision.

The amount of conscious weighing up undertaken will depend on the import of the decision to be made. Ask someone in the office, "Will you spare time for a drink at lunchtime so that we can discuss the next scheduled departmental meeting?" and they may hardly need to think about it at all. It is only a short period; they have to have a bite to eat anyway; and they already know about the meeting and want to be involved. Ask about something more substantial and the weighing up process will involve more, maybe much more.

If you want to define persuasion, it is perhaps best described as being a process of helping people weigh something up and make a decision about it. Literally, when you aim to persuade, you are *helping people decide*. It follows therefore that you need to understand how they actually go about this process. In simple terms, paraphrasing

---

*Note: this section reflects the greater detail given in another book in this *Smart Skills Series*, *Persuasion* by Patrick Forsyth.

psychologists who have studied it, this thinking process can be described thus, people:

- Consider the factors that make up a case.
- Seek to categorise these as advantages or disadvantages.
- Weigh up the complete case, allowing all the pluses and minuses.
- Select a course of action (which may be simply agreeing or not, or involve the choice of one action being taken rather than another), which reflects the overall picture.

Let us be clear. What is going on here is not a search for perfection. Most things we look at have some downsides; this may be the most useful book you ever read, but reading it does take a little time and that could be used for something else. To have this time taken up might well be seen as a downside, whereas its practical use an upside.

An analogy of a pair of old-fashioned weighing scales is worth keeping in mind. It can act as a practical tool, helping you envisage what is going on during what is intended to be a persuasive exchange. Beyond that it helps structure the process if you also have a clear idea of the sequence of thinking involved in this weighing up process.

The thinking process

One way of look at what is going on, is to think of people moving through several stages of thinking, as it were saying to themselves:

- *I matter most.* Whatever you want me to do, I expect you to worry about how I feel about it, respect me and consider my needs.
- *What are the merits and implications of the case you make?* Tell me what you suggest and why it makes sense (the pluses) and whether it has any snags (the minuses) so that I can weigh it up; bearing in mind that few, if any, propositions are perfect.
- *How will it work?* Here people additionally want to assess the details not so much about the proposition itself but about the areas associated with it. For example, you might want to persuade someone to take on, or become involved with, a project. The idea of the project might appeal, but say it ends with them having to prepare a lengthy written report, they might see that as a chore and

therefore as a minus, and might, if the case is finely balanced, reject becoming involved because of that.
- *What do I do?* In other words what action – exactly – is now necessary? This too forms part of the balance. If something seen in a quick flick through this book persuaded you that it might help you, you may have bought it. In doing so you recognised (and accepted) that you would have to read it and that this would take a little time. The action – reading – is inherent in the proposition and, if you were not prepared to take it on, this might have changed your decision.

It is after this thinking is complete that people will feel they have sufficient evidence on which to make a decision. They have the balance in mind, and they can compare it with that of any other options (and remember, some choices are close run with one option only just coming out ahead of others). Then people can decide; feel they have made a sensible decision, and done so on a considered basis.

This thinking process is largely universal. It may happen very quickly and might be almost instantaneous – the snap judgement. Or it may take longer, and that may sometimes indicate days or weeks (or longer!) rather than minutes or hours. But it is always in evidence. Because of this, there is always merit in setting out your case in a way that sits comfortably alongside the way in which it will be considered. Hence: the definition that describes persuasion as *helping the decision-making process*.

This thinking process should not be difficult to identify with; it is what you do too, for instance when you shop. The core of what is necessary when attempting to persuade is to keep it in mind and address the individual questions in turn. So you need to:

- First demonstrate a focus on the other person – it helps also to aim to create some rapport and make clear how you aim to put things over (making clear, for example, how you plan to go through something).
- Then present a balanced case – you need to stress the positive, of course, but not to pretend there are no snags, especially if manifestly there are some, so present a clear case, give it

sufficient explanation and weight and recognise the balancing up that the recipient will undertake.
- Add in working details – mention how things will work, include ancillary details, especially those that will matter to others.

Because of this thinking, when you set out a case the structure and logic of it should sensibly follow this pattern. Otherwise the danger is that you will be trying to do one thing while the person you are communicating with is doing something else. They will do what they want and your job is to keep them on the track that you see as the best route.

Persuasion's magic formula

There is, if not quite a magic formula, certainly one core principle that can help make your every message more persuasive. This is the concept of what are called benefits. People do not buy products and services, and the same goes for ideas or anything else, they buy what these things do for or mean to them. I do not want a laptop computer for its own sake, but I do want to be able to write quickly and easily on the move. Features of the machine, that is its size, weight, portability, battery life and so on, are not ends in themselves; they are only interesting or relevant because of how they produce benefits. Thus the low weight makes the machine portable, which means that I can stick it in my briefcase and write on an aeroplane journey (long battery life is a benefit there too) and the increased productivity (or perhaps greater earnings) are the ultimate benefit.

The relationship here is important. Benefits are made possible or produced by features and if they are relevant to someone then telling them about them is the best core content for a persuasive message. Benefits may be:

- **Tangible or intangible** (in the computer example the status of being seen to have the latest and lightest machine may be as important to some people as the more tangible benefit of several hours work being done while travelling abroad).
- **Personal** (it is valuable to me to be able to work on the move).
- **Corporate** (it is profitable to my company for me to be able to work on the move)

- **Important to other people** someone is concerned about (perhaps I am buying laptops for me and other members of staff and their feelings are important too).

Benefits must always be relevant. Strictly speaking, the fact that a car has a 6-speed gearbox (feature), which will make it more economic and less costly to run (the benefit saves money), is only an advantage if running costs actually matter. Someone buying an expensive sports car may be in a position not to care.

The task here therefore is first to look at the case you plan to make, and to analyse it in terms of its features and benefits. If you list things (benefits on the right as they should most often be stated first, features on the left) then you will see how they interlock. One feature can produce several benefits (as the car's 6-speed gearbox is instrumental in producing a number of things: better fuel economy, less wear and tear on the engine at high speeds and less noise too). Then you can think about how you describe them. If a benefit is put over in truly descriptive terms then it becomes that much stronger in how it can positively affect your case.

Benefits in action

Thus, you could say something will save you money (saving something you want to save is always a benefit, as is gaining anything positive), or that it will not only save money but also recoup its cost in a month, or it will halve what you spend. If the description matches the circumstances of the other party and if it specifically rings bells because of how it is described then this will work best. Consider a product example. A company sells cookery equipment to restaurants and cafes. One product is a flat grill. One feature is its size, there are various models and one has a cooking surface of 800 square centimetres. What is the benefit? It will cook a dozen eggs or six steaks simultaneously. Now most people find it difficult to conjure up 800 square centimetres in their mind's eye, but everyone who runs a restaurant will be able to imagine the eggs and steaks with no problem at all. Link the way this is described to their situation further – "Imagine the rush you get at breakfast time ..." – and it makes a powerful point.

If you always keep in mind what something does for or means to other people you will be able to put over a more powerful case. The phrase "benefit-led" is used in selling and that is a good way of thinking about it. Benefits come first, features explain how that is possible and, if necessary, you can add additional credibility (that is evidence or proof – something other than you saying it's good).

For example: a companion book in this *Smart Skill Series* is called *Persuasion* by Patrick Forsyth (the title is a *feature*). But if it will help you make a persuasive case and obtain agreement from others, that's a *benefit*, and this in turn will save arguments and get more done, *further benefit*. Its methods are tried and tested and their presentation in training courses has received positive feedback (*evidence, to which might be added a positive comment from a named delegate or training organisation*). The idea of teasing out the way you put things by saying "which means that ..." and seeing where that takes you is a good one; start with a feature and at the end of the line you will assuredly have come to a benefit, maybe more than one.

Incidentally, proof – some evidence that is objective (i.e. not just you saying that it is good) – is an important component of the argument. Never rely solely on your own say so, but seek and build in evidence. This could be sheer numbers (thousands of customers can't be wrong), or tests, guarantees or standards met or complied with. We touched earlier on a car as an example. If the distributor says the car will do 50 miles per gallon, do you believe them, or assume that some exaggeration may be involved? How about if they say independent tests in a certain motoring magazine show it does 50mpg? No contest.

You can do worse than list all the things that people might obtain from your offering ahead of speaking to them. Some may be classic (see below), others may be more individual to whatever you are dealing with.

What's in it for me?
As a result of agreeing with you, people might be able to:

- Make more money
- Save money
- Save time, effort or hassle
- Be more secure

- Sort out problems
- Be able to exploit opportunities
- Motivate others (e.g. staff)
- Impress people (e.g. customers)

Your chosen manner

Now with the core aspects that make your case in mind, you need to think more about how to put it over. The way your message is approached is also important. For example, if, as soon as you have said even a few words, it is clear that you are taking it for granted that agreement will follow and if this seems inappropriately arrogant then the likelihood is that it will not be taken so seriously.

The approach taken to putting over your case should be:

- **Well considered**: if it has clearly been put over without thought the case will be given less credence.
- **Well projected**: it should have the courage of its convictions; everything about the way it is expressed – language, style and argument – should add to its power.
- **Empathetic**: in other words it should come over as respecting other peoples' points of view and seeing things from their perspective.

Empathy is perhaps especially important. If it is well in evidence it prevents other elements – however persuasively put – coming over as unreasonable or "pushy". A balanced approach is necessary here. If everything is piled on to create more and more persuasive power, then the message becomes strident and what is being done becomes self-defeating. If persuasion is tempered with empathy then the whole point becomes more acceptable.

If persuasion follows these principles then already it has a better chance of succeeding. It is worth remembering that:

- It helps to think of persuasion as helping people to decide.
- Your logic must therefore reflect theirs.
- The essence of being persuasive is to make it easy for people to make a decision, and do so in a way that makes your suggested action seem the best choice.

LINKING TO NEGOTIATION

If you have communicated clearly and achieved understanding, if you have succeeded in being truly persuasive and there is essentially agreement to proceed, then you can move on to the process of negotiation; indeed it is only at this stage that the other party will be willing to get into the details that negotiation demands and acts to sort out and agree.

You need to remember that the processes of persuasion and negotiation overlap. There is no sharp division. Often a complete cycle of interaction takes place, as was described earlier, with communication going on throughout the piece. While the approach described, operating from the basis of a sound appreciation of the other person's point of view, is the beginning of being effective in this area, there is clearly more to it than that. The process of communication needs working at and that of persuasive communication even more so. It must be made manageable. It needs planning and structuring. The process must be deployed with an acute consciousness of what is going on, because you never know how people will react.

There is a balance to be struck if both parties are to come out of the ensuing exchange satisfactorily, and it is best if people avoid reacting precipitously or emotionally and see the situation for what it is: negotiation. If their discussions take this approach then a solution is likely to be satisfactory to everyone. Situations can be mishandled as much by failure to negotiate as by negotiating badly.

Two key factors to making negotiation work for you are:

- **Understanding** how negotiation relates to communication generally, and to persuasive communication in particular, so that you can make everything play its part.
- **Recognising** that communicating clearly is an important component of negotiation; in fact no negotiation is possible if one party does not understand exactly what the other is saying.

It is this that underlies everything else you do and helps make your negotiating effective; and there is a good deal more with which to get to grips. So, having set the scene, we move on to specific techniques.

Chapter 1

NEGOTIATION:
Getting to grips with the core approaches

> 'I love negotiating. It's creative. I love the feeling of seeing something and saying "I can do something with this".'
> *Phillipe Edmonds*

Negotiating can be deceptive in that there may be more to it than at first meets the eye. Consider what negotiation is not. It is not simply stating a grievance. Imagine that your watch has come back from the menders and is still only doing a good job of telling you the time on the planet Mercury (where a day lasts 59 Earth days). It would be most people's instinct to complain, but often without proposing any remedy. At best, complaints produce apologies. At worst, they produce arguments in which threats produce counter-threats, and this can ultimately result in an impasse. All too often communication can end up this way.

It starts with a complaint: "productivity in your department is dropping, sales results are below target", and deteriorates into an argument: "No, it's not", "There are good reasons for that" ... and so on. What you really want in such circumstances is action. You have to suggest, or prompt, a proposal: something that will put things right. Arguments cannot be negotiated, only proposals can.

This, in turn, demands that emotions are kept under control. Always remember that negotiation is a delicate business, one which needs thinking about carefully both before and during the process.

The win-win concept

It is inherent to the process of negotiation that *both* the parties involved end up feeling satisfied that an appropriate deal has been struck. It may not be exactly the result they hoped for, but it is one they can realistically agree to. It is this outcome that gives rise to the description of what is called a "win-win" negotiating situation. Thus: win-win negotiation recognises the realities of the process and accepts that matters must end with some degree of satisfaction for both parties, especially when one negotiation lays the foundations for further ones.

Some individuals feel they must win every point, deliberately aiming to create a "win-lose" approach. Always remember that negotiation is a process of some give and take, and that if both parties accept this then a win-win approach is more likely to achieve a productive conclusion. Consider the implications. For instance, to achieve a win-win outcome you must:

- Put the emphasis on seeking common ground, rather than fighting for your way on everything.
- Relate to the other party and their concerns, rather than just objecting to them.
- Have a readiness to compromise, at least to some degree, rather than remaining inflexible.
- Allow discussion to accommodate to and fro debate, rather than insisting on a rigid agenda.
- Ensure discussion includes questioning – and thus listening – rather than just giving statements of your case.
- Disclose appropriate information, rather than maintaining total secretiveness.
- Build relationships, rather than bad feelings with other people to smooth the way.
- Aim for agreement and not stalemate.

A win-win conclusion should normally be your aim. Complexities demand care. Several elements need to be borne in mind if the process is to move along satisfactorily. Overall: negotiation is the process of identifying, arranging and agreeing the terms and conditions, whatever they may be, of a deal.

Initially persuasive communication is where one party puts across their case and, in their own mind, the other person begins to accept it even if nothing is tacitly said at this stage. As agreement in principle begins to emerge the question switches from "Will this person agree?" to "On what basis will they agree?" Each party is then concerned that every detail making up the deal will suit them as much as possible. It may be impossible for both to be satisfied 100% on every factor; indeed this probably will not be the case, but the balance must be right.

NEGOTIATION IS TRADING

The different factors that must be agreed during negotiation are called *variables*. They may indeed be many and various, and this fact contributes to the overall complexity of the negotiation process.

Let's illustrate the point. Imagine you are going to make some major household purchase: a refrigerator, perhaps. Which model you buy, and from where, will depend on a number, perhaps a surprisingly large number of factors – variables. There is price, of course. But there are also factors about the fridge itself: the star rating of its freezer unit, the size, number and arrangements of shelves, bottle-holding capacity, the colour, which way the door opens, and so on. There may be other, less obvious factors. How much does it cost to run? Will they deliver it, by when and with what certainty? Will they carry it up to a third floor apartment? What payment terms are available? What guarantee and service arrangements apply? You can no doubt think of more.

This kind of purchase may consist only of checking and considering such factors and then making a decision, but some of the factors may not be fixed. Some will be offered – or not – by the supplier, others have to be suggested and negotiated. Only when something has been raised, discussed and agreed can it become part of the deal.

A balance is necessary here. Both parties may need to give as well as take. You agree to delay delivery by two weeks and they will deliver free of charge when they have a van coming your way. They agree to knock, say, 10% off the price if you agree to pay cash. And so on. In other words, you trade variables. You swap aspects of them to balance and re-balance the deal. Such trading may use all or part of a variable: for instance, you might agree to collect the fridge, foregoing any kind of delivery, but in return for a greater discount. Of course some options and decisions preclude negotiating: buy from a website, for instance, and the price may be right but the rest of the deal is usually fixed.

A key principle to keep in mind is that understanding, identifying, assessing and trading variables are at the core of negotiation and are what, above all, can get you a good deal (we look at just how we work with this a little later).

The jigsaw pieces of negotiation.
Variables are the jigsaw pieces of the negotiation process. Each one has a scale of possible decisions on which you must settle and agree. For example:

- *Discount*: none or 50%.
- *Delivery*: this afternoon at exactly 3pm, this week, next week, sometime ...

There are often many variables; you need a clear idea about what position on the scale is likely to be acceptable to both sides, and the relative importance of different ones. The more variables there are, and the harder they are to prioritise, and the more complex the negotiation becomes, the human interactions inherent in the process complicate the negotiation.

MAXIMISING THE LIKELIHOOD OF SUCCESS
Try to wing it and you may look back after a meeting and conclude you lost out. Perhaps you failed to recognise the need for negotiation. If such an underestimate is made, then any transaction will be handled inadequately and the end result is likely to be a bad deal. For example, an administration manager may telephone a supplier to complain about an incorrectly completed service on a company car. A complaint may produce no more than an apology. If the manager wants something done about it he or she must suggest a remedy – maybe balancing the inconvenience of the car going back in with the seriousness of any fault and the option of leaving it until the next service.

There are many different approaches possible here, and very different arrangements may result from them. If you see something as negotiation, but go at it like a bull at a gate, or focus exclusively on a single element or allow the transaction to develop into an argument, you are unlikely to achieve mutual agreement.

Three interrelated fundamentals are important:

- **What you do.** The techniques and processes of all sorts that are involved.
- **The manner you adopt.** The manner you employ and the effects this has on those with whom you negotiate.
- **Preparation.** The first two fundamentals are both dependent on this one. Given the complexities already mentioned, preparing for negotiation is no more than common sense. Yet it is easier said than done. Probably more negotiators fail to reach the best arrangement for want of adequate preparation than for any other reason.

A positive approach is essential; so, remember the old saying quoted earlier: you don't get what you deserve, you get what you negotiate. Success does, of course, have to be earned. It was Vidal Sassoon who said: "The only place where success comes before work is in the dictionary." Making negotiation work, as in so much else in life, does not just happen. People with good skills in this area tend to make it look easy. A good cook or a skilful public speaker make what they do seem effortless, but this does not mean that a good deal of preparation has not been necessary for this impression to be given. Accepting that some preparation is always necessary, however long or short the process may need to be, is the first step to deploying the right approach.

Getting a step ahead

In many kinds of negotiation no quarter is given. For instance, think of the vehemence of some international negotiations between nations, or of certain wage-bargaining situations. A great deal may hang on the outcome and the negotiator needs to have every trick of the trade on their side in order to create an edge. Despite the complexities involved, things should be already be starting to fall into place.

Anyone with whom you negotiate is likely to apply pressure to get the best deal. They will be intent on fighting their corner, meeting their objectives, financial or otherwise, and will do their best for their own position – not yours. Never underestimate the skill or resolve of those with whom you negotiate; if you assume anything let it be that you need to pull out all the stops. To do that there is something basic and straightforward that helps – you must make sure that you are well prepared. If preparation sounds like a bit of a chore, take heart: it pays to do your homework and sound preparation can give you your first edge in negotiation; an edge that can make all the difference to the outcome.

Chapter 2

PREPARATION:
The route to achieving success

'If you are not planning where you want to be, what reason or excuse do you have for worrying about being nowhere?'
Tom Hopkins

Again, do not regard preparation as a chore. It's not; attempting to wing it is likely to put your whole strategy in jeopardy. Preparation is an essential preliminary to success. So, if that is so, the next question concerns how to go about preparing to negotiate. Do you think of yourself as inexperienced at – and perhaps even wary of – the process of negotiation? If so, this is, at least in part, doubtless only because you are still to some degree ill-prepared for doing it. Being well-prepared breeds confidence, and that alone will help you boost your expertise. Confidence allows the process to be better managed than an *ad hoc* approach ever can be. In addition, appearing confident will be read by others as competence; the way you appear is very important, as we will explore later.

The process of getting well-prepared may constitute just a few moments' thought prior to the start of a conversation. It may be a few minutes, or an hour or two of homework. Or it may mean sitting round the table with colleagues, thrashing out the best way forward and sometimes even rehearsing what will be done. Whatever scale of preparation circumstances dictate, the nature of the negotiation process means it *must always* take place – it can give you what others may feel is an "unfair" advantage, one that stands you in good stead throughout the process.

FOCUSING ON OTHER PEOPLE
Sound preparation needs to consider two interrelated factors:

- The other people involved
- Your own position.

As you prepare you must first consider the person (or people) with whom you must negotiate and, if appropriate, the organisation they represent. Negotiation may take place with all sorts of people: customers, suppliers, business colleagues (or your boss, or subordinates) and with people you may or may not know personally. Questions need to be answered about such people, for example what:

- Role and/or intentions do they have?
- Needs (subjective and objective) do they have?
- What problems will they raise? What objections will they make?
- What are they aiming to achieve and how strong is their bargaining position?
- Can they decide alone and what must they consult about with someone else?

Every negotiation will raise different issues, but the principle of thinking through how people may handle something is similar in each case. Do not overlook this, or assume familiarity makes it unnecessary. Even with people you know and deal with regularly, such analysis may pay dividends. Two elements are important here.

The topic of negotiation
First, what the negotiation is about is clearly important. For example, consider negotiating regarding meeting accommodation. Suppose you are making arrangements with the banquet manager at a hotel or conference centre to accommodate the annual general meeting of your

organisation. You want it to go well. You want the arrangements to be appropriate. You want it to be memorable. The banquet manager wants it to go well too, of course, but they are also concerned that it should fit in with other functions, be easy to staff and be profitable. For your part you must be sure the banquet manager has sufficient authority to make the arrangements you want, that the person is professional, knowledgeable, and that what they say will be possible will prove to be so. Suppose a combination of rooms A and B is suggested. You feel B and C would suit better. Is their suggestion based on how your group will be best accommodated, or to allow the fitting in of the local football club in room C? And do you want them next door anyway? As each element such as cost and catering is discussed and various options reviewed, your knowledge of the banquet manager and their intentions will allow you to negotiate more successfully with them than if you knew nothing about them. The two of you may never have met before, but some consideration of what they are likely to be feeling and planning will always help.

The people
Secondly, people – all of whom are different. Everyone is an individual and you must deal with any number of differences between you and those with whom you negotiate. Any difference may be significant, but let's look at an example where the differences may be marked, that of cross cultural negotiation.

For instance, the Japanese use the word "Yes" (Hai) not only to mean yes, but just as likely to mean "I'm listening", "Right", "I see", "Understood" and more. They avoid the word "No" (Lai) in order not to offend, so rather than say "No" it is more likely to be something like "Let's look at this further". If they really want to express a negative then the most likely word to be used is "Difficult". And that is just a few words in two languages! The moral is simple: forewarned is forearmed and if you negotiate in multi-cultural situations you need to do your homework. Let us be clear. Negotiation demands that we:

- "Read" people to try and identify their attitude and position at any particular point in the proceedings.

- Anticipate what may occur and what line people may take as things progress.
- Match what you do to the precise state that the other party is in at the time.

All the above are, in turn, dependent on clear understanding, and all this may be different – and perhaps more difficult – with someone of different outlook or experience. We may recognise the fact, but responding to it still needs conscious effort and the problem is one of what is called expectation. We grow up through a multitude of experiences and all of them are used, semi-automatically, to predict how the future will be; it is a process that gives you an expectation. For example, if you are asked to a dinner party or a cocktail party then you may well believe that, broadly at least, you know how it will be. Certainly you know something about how prompt you should be in attending, what you should and should not wear, how you should conduct yourself, and so on. Normally too, at least in your own environment, your expectation will be broadly correct.

But in unfamiliar circumstances – in negotiating with a foreign buyer, say – your expectation of many things can be either wrong or murky. You have to remain open-minded and plan to be quick on your feet so that you can try to respond appropriately even as you quickly learn how things are going to be. Clearly any checking, research or briefing you can undertake in advance will be an asset. It enables you to deal with the situation better, it prevents you making real gaffes and it may give you an edge over colleagues or adversaries who have taken less trouble and are therefore less well briefed.

A number of factors are worth bearing in mind. Taking the foreign buyer example further, such include, in no particular order:

- **Language:** although English is to a large extent the universal language of business, those whose first language is English still need to exercise some caution in dealing with those for whom it is not. For example:
  – Speak a little slower than normal: though not so slowly as to sound patronising.
  – Be careful and precise in your use of language: to ensure

accurate meaning is transferred, consider restricting vocabulary a little.

– Signpost clearly: that is be sure to say what is coming and the nature of it: "Let me give you an example", "an important point is …"

– Verify understanding as you go: again do not overdo it, but an occasional remark like "Am I making that clear?" is useful. Note: if discussions are being translated special care is necessary and it is worthwhile to discuss how it will be done with the translator ahead of the main discussion.

- **Beginnings**: be particularly careful about introductions and greetings, things like eye contact (not too long at first in the Middle East, and not with women) and not flinching from a Russian bear hug can be important.
- **Appearance**: this is largely a matter of common sense, though if you are taken out it may be worth checking what is appropriate in advance.
- **Manners**: this can be something of a minefield; you may need to find out whether you need to eat the sheep's eyes in the Middle East and know that it is rude to cross your legs and point your feet at someone in a Buddhist country. Just the appropriate level of familiarity needs checking; the French for instance tend to be more formal than most people and "Monsieur/Madam" need to be used regularly. Equally you must not be unnecessarily offended by, say, the Chinese who can be very abrupt as a matter of course, "No, that's wrong!", without meaning it quite as it would be taken if put that way in the West.
- **Body language**: the signs given in another culture may be confusing. In Bulgaria, a nodded head means disagreement and nodding means agreement; in Korea, too much smiling is taken as someone being pushy.
- **Humour**: careful! It may not travel; too much may be seen as inappropriately frivolous, but on the other hand you probably do not want to come over as too serious in some circumstances.
- **Timing**: attitudes to time vary widely. Punctuality has different degrees of importance around the world; indeed there are countries in which this is radically different (I have waited more than an hour for someone in Thailand, for instance and the delay

has not even been commented on). More importantly, some cultures just take longer over some things. In America the culture is very much one of "getting down to business"; elsewhere, in the East for instance, preliminaries are important and taking time just to get to know each other a little is regarded as normal.

Even tiny details may matter. For example, Americans write the date: 12-15-11, i.e. with the month first. In Britain it is usually the reverse. Certainly this needs getting right before you agree a deadline. Matters to do with every day things may cause problems too. Take meal times: if you dine in Japan it is likely to be early (6/7pm), with an Italian it will be late (9/10pm) – getting this kind of detail wrong can offend.

As relationships grow, perhaps if you are meeting and doing business regularly, a wider set of circumstances needs to be taken into account and planned for – entertaining, for example. Whether you are travelling to other parts of the world, or dealing with people who travel to you, some care in all these ways is sensible. Certainly it is important not to stereotype people or make assumptions; and this is easy to do when your experience of something is limited.

A case in point

Here, just to illustrate the range of things to be borne in mind, let's consider one country, albeit one that is alien to many, returning again to Japan. Japanese business people tend to be well-travelled, are group orientated and rather formal in their dealings with each other. To get off to a good start in negotiations with Japanese you should: not overdo eye contact, shake hands only if a hand is offered to you (and *do not* try to bow in Japanese style, though a sincere nod of the head is appreciated), use titles with names and make sure that careful use of language ensures understanding – checking as necessary. Business cards are much used (yours should have a Japanese translation on the reverse).

Details may be widely checked. If you quote a delivery date, they will want to speak to those involved in implementing it to reassure themselves that it is seen as possible. The Japanese go to considerable lengths to conceal their emotions, hate losing face, and are uncomfortable if others (you) lose control, for instance showing anger or impatience. Respect and patience are to be displayed and any negotiation is, in part, seen as a pursuit of harmony.

Language will always need to be used carefully and you should not act immediately to fill silences, as taking a moment over things is normal. Politeness and consideration is valued, and personal touches (things like a thank you note, or small gifts – which you should make before unwrapping if one is given to you) are seen as very much part of building relationships.

Specifically in negotiation: considerable detail is expected about any matter being discussed. An overview or seemingly vague or disorganised information will be read with suspicion as evasion. Good support material – anything from plans and graphs to summaries of details dealt with – is appreciated, indeed expected. As Japanese people will most likely deal with you as a group, it is unusual to deal with a single person, you must relate to the whole group, even those taking less part or less able to speak English (if that is the language being used). The differences here, certainly compared to a Western approach, are considerable, and even a snapshot like this is sufficient to show that a good deal of checking is necessary and likely to pay dividends.

Such a picture can quickly be used to flesh out a plan of action. Specific factors may be necessary:

- Allowing a longer time than would be necessary elsewhere.
- More thorough preparation (for example to be able to express the necessary detail in a succinct and logical form).
- Research to get details about the people who will be involved.
- Having available – in advance – any gifts and certainly appropriate and tailored support material that may be desirable.

All that said, and much of this example simply hints at a bigger picture, such factors are a separate and parallel dimension to everything else that is important about negotiation. Whatever culture you may deal with, some research and planning is likely to be useful – as then are all the other principles that act to help make negotiation successful. Always remember that you will *never* know or understand as much about a nation or particular culture as those for whom it is "theirs". You need to recognise that you can go on learning and not allow yourself to come to a point where you think you know it all.

It may surprise you when you make your umpteenth visit to a particular country and things still happen that cast just a little more light on how things work there. If you are open-minded then this process will never stop; and every incidence of it can help make your next negotiation more successful.

The cultural example is just one aspect. The need for some consideration and the adoption of a suitable approach is true of whoever you deal with in whatever circumstances. There is value in knowing your adversary as it were, and thus value too in some checking of their nature, what is likely to be important to them and how they are likely to handle matters.

A further factor: you

The other party involved is, of course, you. How you are seen is important, too. People will respect you more if they feel you appear professional, or expert, if you clearly have the authority to negotiate, if you appear prepared, confident and in charge. You may never be quite as close to this ideal as you would like, but often the other person has no way of knowing this and "appear" is indeed the right word. Some people seem to have the confidence to tell you black is white and make you believe it. The exception to this is appearing prepared. You must, as has been said, actually be prepared, though it may well do no harm to appear even better prepared than you actually are. The need to think matters through thoroughly is thus essential.

CLEAR OBJECTIVES

The need to have objectives firmly in mind is perhaps obvious, but surely there is no problem in making them clear? But if you simply say, "I want the best deal possible", then this provides nothing tangible with which to work. There is all the difference in the world between an author saying, "Let's see if the magazine editor will pay me more for my next article" and setting out to obtain a 10% increase in the fee.

Returning to the example of the company annual meeting, here too making objectives clear is an important starting point. Briefly, the objectives for the annual company meeting might effectively be stated as:

- Being successful (and this might be defined in detail);
- Everyone feeling it to be appropriate in style and purpose;
- Being memorable and impressive: setting the scene for the year to come.

What else? What about cost? Are these objectives regardless of cost or do they have to be achieved within a budget? What about equipment and visual aids? This introduces another area of variables, and another scale against which matters must be judged and settled. The answer might be that the objectives are certainly not regardless of cost, but that the budget must be realistic if what is wanted is to be achieved satisfactorily.

Similarly, if visual aids are vital, the date of the meeting itself could be changed to secure a larger and better equipped meeting room, where the right equipment can easily be accommodated and a more professional show can be put on.

Objective setting: a systematic approach

Ahead of any negotiation you need to identify and set clear objectives. You need to have your priorities clear, and clearly related to what variables are involved, and understand your attitude to each. For example, are there some variables about which you are prepared to compromise and, if so, how far? And are there others about which you intend to be immovable? One such factor might be timing. For instance, do you intend to achieve everything at once, in one meeting, or is a long term strategy involved?

The purpose of whatever you plan to negotiate about and however it is to be done must be clear. You must be able to answer the question "Why am doing this?" And set out a clear purpose, one that always needs to involve both you and whoever you are to negotiate with and that describes what effect you aim to have on them and what outcome should ideally result. Objectives need not only to be clear, but spelt out in sufficient detail (certainly in your own mind and sometimes for others who may be involved with you). They must act to provide genuine guidance to what you will do. They also need to reflect not just what you want, but recognise the two-sided nature of negotiation.

To spell out exactly what objectives must encompass, consider a much-quoted acronym which provides a good guide: **SMART**. This stands for:

Specific
　Measurable
　　Achievable
　　　Realistic
　　　　Timed.

As an example, you might regard objectives linked to say making a formal presentation, as being to:

- Enable you to ensure your presentations come over in future in a way that audiences will see as appropriate and informative (**specific**).
- Ensure (**measurable**) action takes place afterwards (here you might link to any appropriate measure: from agreements or actions that group members take or commit to, to the volume of applause received!).
- Be right for them: providing sufficient, understandable information in manageable form that really allows them to change and improve what is prompted later (an **achievable** result).
- Be **realistic**, that is desirable – hence having a reasonable duration in mind, one that people are likely to see as appropriate.
- Provide **timing**; always a good factor to include in any objective. If your presentation is designed to prompt action, then when are you aiming for that to be taken? At the end or a year later?

Even before you even begin to prepare you should ask yourself whether you are clear in this respect. If you know *why* the negotiation is to happen and *what* you intend to *achieve*, then you are well on the way to making it work. Thus time spent sorting this, and making sure you have a clear vision of what the objectives are, is time well spent. It may only take a few moments, but is still worth doing. Or it may need more thought and take more time. So be it. It is still worth doing and in any case may well save time on later stages of your preparatory thinking.

Thinking through what your objectives are is not an academic issue; your clarity and surety about them help you conduct the kind of meeting that will help you reach them. Remember, with preparation in mind, that: ready, aim, fire is always likely to be the best order in which to work!

GIVING THE MEETING APPROPRIATE STRUCTURE

The thinking above is designed to influence the way in which a meeting will work. In fact, your preparation should anticipate something of all the factors that make up the complexities of negotiation. Preparation also includes matters relevant to the topic with which the negotiation is bound up. For example, you may need to think how arguments can be justified as your point of view is explained. This goes back to general communication and any particular focus it may have – for example, the need to be persuasive. As you have seen, the variable factors of negotiation are, in effect, traded. You may find the jargon here confusing, as some people use "variable" and "concession" almost interchangeably. In fact, while all variables may be traded, not all may be used as concessions in the sense of giving something away. More of this process later: but here the only point to make is that you will handle this give-and-take process much better if you have thought through some of the – perhaps many – options.

Continuing to refer to the example of the company annual meeting, the organiser might deal with the Banquet Manager thus, saying: "If we start an hour later, and choose an alternative menu, can we have the larger room at the same cost?" Here three elements: timing, menu and room options are being used together in relation to overall cost and are referred to within a sentence.

Negotiation can get very much more complicated than that, hence the need to have a firm logical structure and sequence to keep everything under control during a meeting. By structure I mean the shape and to some extent the style of the meeting. Structure encompasses everything that will avoid any sort of muddle, for example, what do you envisage happening? What will you aim to do first, second and third? Having a clear and logical structure in mind helps you keep control of the meeting and of all the disparate elements that you bring to the table.

Consideration needs to be given to the likely, or planned, duration of the meeting. For example, do you have one hour for discussion, several hours, or must everything be agreed more promptly? Your order of sequence and priority must fit within the duration of the meeting. You will need to be very clear which are primary and which are secondary matters. If time runs short you do not want to find you have omitted anything of primary concern. A well written report has a beginning, a middle and end; so does a good presentation. Both may require a detailed structure within each main segment, however, and a negotiation meeting is just the same.

Manner and feeling
You need not only to think about what you want to do; you also need to think of how you want a meeting to go in terms of manner and feeling. For example, there may be stages at which you wish to be seen as particularly reasonable, or the opposite, and stages when you need to come over with some real heavyweight clout. What kind of personal profile do you wish to project? Make sure that your negotiating style is not in conflict with this. One should enhance the other.

It is not the role of preparation to cast what you intend to do in tablets of stone. You must retain a degree of flexibility throughout. You can never know for sure what the other party will do, but a clear plan still helps. It sets out your intention: what you would like to do. Think of your plan like a route map, not a straightjacket. Good planning should not prevent you being flexible and responding to circumstances. Indeed it makes it easier to do so. On a journey, a route map does not prevent you from changing your route if you unexpectedly find roadworks in the way. Indeed the map helps you both divert and get back on track.

Successful negotiation does not just happen; nor does the detail of how a meeting needs to progress. As you review the conduct of negotiation, both the shape of the meeting and the detail within that shape will become clearer. So, you should remember that:

- Negotiation involves more than one party; a win-win approach tends to produce the best result for both.
- Variables are the raw material of negotiating and success rests to a large extent on how you handle them. If you do not know where you are going, it is difficult to proceed with precision, so setting clear objectives is a prerequisite part of planning and preparation.

So you should prepare carefully, both what you will do and how you will do it, and take a view of both sides of the situation. Preparation provides a clear way forward; to quote a classic business maxim – if you don't know where you are going, any road will do. It is a process that must not be skimped and assessing the variables is an important part of it. You need to:

- Identify what variables your own negotiation meetings involve. These must be worked out in advance for any meeting you are to be involved in
- Check whether you are overlooking any possibilities.
- Work out, realistically, what preparation you must do and what form it needs to take.

Everything must be thought through, for instance consider whether involving a colleague who can act as a sounding board could be useful. Preparation may sensibly involve making some notes to guide you through. You may want to keep these hidden from the person with whom you are negotiating, but if a check of points to be made will be useful then do have the necessary details to hand during the meeting. One example of this is calculations: it can be impressive if, anticipating something as you plan, you can then glance (unobtrusively) at your notes during the meeting and say something like, I don't think 13.5% does the trick, that's only £12,000 ...

Do not underestimate the time you need to set aside to prepare or how useful doing so can be. At the risk of repetition, the prime rule about preparation is simply *always to do it*.

Chapter 3

TRADING
Achieving successful balance

*'There are some men who in a fifty-fifty proposition
insist on getting the hyphen too.'*
Laurence J Peter

Variables and the trading of them may be at the core of the negotiating process, but they are not all identical – they differ both in nature and potential. Similarly, their roles in trading may vary. Linking them to your plan and objectives will show you their potential role in the subsequent proceedings.

DIFFERENT CATEGORIES OF VARIABLE
Three types of variable are usually highlighted, they are:

- **The loss leaders**: Loss leaders take their name from products sold at nil or negative profit margins simply to attract buyers; the buyers then create profit by purchasing other products on their visit. In negotiation it refers to those aspects you are really prepared to trade with, even if you would prefer not to, in order to clinch a deal. You need to regard some things as being in this category.
- **The ideals**: Those factors which you would like to achieve and

which would constitute the ideal deal. Realistically these must include factors around which you are prepared to make some compromise.
- **The must haves**: Those factors you feel you must take from the negotiation if the deal is to be at all acceptable to you.

If all you do is state an unchangeable position and refuse to move, the outcome may be permanent stalemate. Some say this was what caused Sir Edward Heath's downfall as UK Prime Minister. During a major miners' strike he did just this. Believing his first offer (from which he refused to deviate) could not, by definition, be his last, the miners dug in their heels. There was effectively no negotiation, and ultimately the government toppled.

HOW TO TRADE VARIABLES

A "ritual" to and fro trading process must be involved; without it stalemate may easily result. The process is literally fundamental to negotiation. With a view of what you have to work with in mind we can now turn to the tactical principles that will help you conduct an effective meeting.

An early start

It is often best to start trading concessions early on in a negotiating meeting. Doing this means that even if they initially reflect peripheral issues, it can still set the scene for what follows. Avoid giving anything – certainly anything significant – away early on. Even saying, "Why don't you talk this through over lunch? My treat," may give the wrong impression. Better to say, "If you agree to come to an agreement today, then I will buy us lunch and you can chat this through in comfort." If this kind of swap is handled informally, then no one need feel boxed in. The conversation can move naturally to a more business-like level. Then the trading can really start and you can use trading variables to get the negotiating process underway and on track.

The rules of trading

Beyond using trading in the form of tentative exploration, as in the example above, it is more powerful done on what might be called an "if you will do this I will do that" basis; indeed, this really must take place for an acceptable balance to be reached. Such exchanges are often prompted by "What if...?" questions; that is a specific aspect of negotiation, the process where adjustments are made by making suggestions that offer new ways of rebalancing matters – "What if ... I do this and you then accept (or do) that?" Complex negotiations involve a good deal of this. "What if ..." questions lead the way to successful trading.

Note: always bear in mind that this is not simply a mechanistic process. Rather it is one strand going on within the total discussion – one utilising a variety of techniques and the careful deployment of various behavioural factors (with everything assisted by judicious preparation), which can make or break your success. Trading must be well executed, but as an integral part of everything done.

Given clear objectives and an overall plan in mind, discussions can proceed. Setting an agenda is sensible for any complex meeting. There is some merit in being the one that suggests one, albeit describing it as something helpful to both parties. If you say something like: "We might find it best to ..." followed by an outline of how you want things to run (though *not*, of course, stating it as helpful to you) this sets the scene. Though it must be borne in mind that doing this has something of a "laying all the cards on the table" feel to it – you may want to judge its precision and comprehensiveness carefully to allow you some flexibility. Alternatively, you may want to take on a more demanding tone at the start.

For every trade made, two important overall rules should always be followed:

1. Never give a concession, trade it reluctantly
The first part (never give) is important because the number of variables is finite and you want your share. The second is too because perception is as important to how things go as fact. You want to be seen to be driving a hard bargain; otherwise you may not be taken seriously; indeed any apparent weakness will be pounced on. Remember the old saying: "If you look like a doormat, people will walk all over you."

2. Optimise or minimise every concession
This means optimising your concessions – talking up their value – and

minimising the value of what they offer you as they are discussed and at and after their acceptance. You can do this in terms of both value and how you talk about them. Try to build up the value, significance and importance of anything you offer and minimise that of what is offered to you.

Let's look at the two sides of this process in turn.

Concession optimisation
The tactic here is to make what you offer seem as valuable as possible, by:

- Stressing the cost (financial or otherwise) to you: "Well, I suppose I could do that but it will involve me in a lot more work."
- Exaggerating, but maintaining credibility. Do not overstate and, if possible, provide evidence. "Well, I could do that but it will involve me in at least twice as much work. I have just been through ..."
- Referring to a major problem which your concession will solve. "I suppose, if I was to agree that, it would remove the need for you to ..."
- Implying that you are making an exceptional concession. "I would never normally do this, but ..."
- Referring to past discussions, and their successful outcome, and what you did for them. "Remember how useful so and so was? I suppose we could go that route again, how about ..." (clearly this is only possible when both parties have prior experience of each other).

Lead-in tactics like this not only build the significance of what you are offering, and make it more acceptable, but also make it more likely to be accepted quickly because there is an implied urgency (something that you may elect to exaggerate where appropriate).

Concessions minimisation
This tactic is to make the other person's offerings seem insignificant (even when you plan to accept their concession), it means:

- Not overdoing the thanks. Not a profuse "Thank you" so much as just a brief, even dismissive, "thanks". This is as much a matter of tone as of the words used.
- Taking it for granted, in fact saying it is not a concession at all but a foregone conclusion: "Fine, I was certainly assuming that …"
- Denying any value: "No, that really doesn't help."
- Devaluing by implying you already have what is being offered; "OK, though I already have …"
- Depreciating them, belittling the value: "Right, that's a small step forward, I guess."
- Amortising them where appropriate. That is, divide them where smaller units will sound less impressive. Thus saying, "Well, at least that would save me X every month", rather than quoting the annual figure.
- Treating them as given and thus of no real value. A brief acknowledgement may be all that is necessary to give this impression: "Right, let's do it that way."
- Accepting, but in doing so implying that you are doing a favour: "I don't really need that, but fine, let's arrange things that way if you think it helps."
- Linking value to time, implying it is now not worth what is implied: "Well, that helps a little, but it isn't of major importance now you've …"

Note: Minimising concessions does not work in every environment. In the Middle East, for instance, the reverse is necessary. Always check local conditions if you have to work overseas – the local culture will doubtless necessitate some finetuning of your approach. Indeed, it is not just culture in the international sense – the culture of an organisation or a specialist group, say of engineers, may be relevant too.

To reinforce this point let me add a couple of acronyms (where would any trainer be without a few acronyms?). The following is an apt reminder of the way such trading must be conducted: ENHANCE and REDUCE:

E – imply that something is **exceptional**
N – refer to a **need** that you are satisfying
H – refer to any previous **history** between you
A – imply that you might be exceeding your **authority**
N – offer your concession as **nourishment** to the relationship
C – stress the cost to you of the **concession**
E – provide **evidence** to build up the value of your concession.

Conversely:

R – **reduce** their concession by the way you speak of it
E – treat it as **expected** and take it for granted
D – **deny** it having any real value
U – **underplay** thanks in both words and tone of voice
C – **contribute** it back to them
E – use **empathy** ("I can see you might think that would help, but ...")

CREATING AN ADVANTAGE
It is a useful tactic, as concessions are either minimised or optimised as appropriate, to trade a concession which in fact costs you little. Though if it has an implied value which brings a relatively more valuable concession in return from the other side, you will gain from the swap.

Such difference in value is one factor that can give you an edge. A concession which you offer, but which you imply is of little or no value, is likely to prompt the offer of a low value concession in return. Thus throughout the process you must play down your thanks for concessions gained and imply their low value, and build up the value of everything that you may concede. The only restraint on this exaggeration is the need to retain the credibility you should be at pains to project.

This whole process is a question of degree. People know there is a ritual to negotiation, but always need to form a judgment of how far this goes.

STEADY AS SHE GOES
The complexities involved can mean that there may be a large number of balls in the air during negotiation. It is something of a juggling trick and keeping track of the variables is quite a task, but you can prepare

for it. If you have thought through what you want to do, and considered the possibilities and anticipated the reaction of the other side, then you will have a picture that you can amend and adapt as discussions proceed. It may help to imagine the variables as boxes of different weights in terms of the image of a weighing scale imagined earlier.

There are real dangers here. If you forget something, or don't deal with it appropriately and at the right time, then it may be impossible to bring it up later; or to do so from a strong position and without displaying uncertainty or weakness. Make sure you have the overall position clearly in mind as you deal with the various points. If you are well organised then anyone less so is at a disadvantage in dealing with you and this can produce another edge for you.

Look for further variables

Your approach must always be a flexible one. Never get locked into previous plans that take you irrevocably in a direction that may no longer be best; remember planning is only a guide. The good negotiator is quick on their feet. Sometimes what happens is very much along the lines you expect, but some finetuning is always necessary and sometimes a great deal needs to be done.

Remember: the saying that "everything is negotiable" can often be true. The moral is to regard keeping searching for variables as an ongoing activity. You may well find that something that has been firmly described as fixed will suddenly come into play. There is merit in remaining open minded to such possibilities and, where appropriate, taking the initiative.

Surfing the Internet, I find a six-year-old girl quoted as saying, "If you want a guinea pig, you start by asking for a pony." If she clearly already has the basis for all this in mind, surely it cannot be too difficult? The problem, if there is one, is with the number of variables (of differing import) with which you must juggle. It is easy to get flustered in the heat of the moment and lose track of what you are trying to do; hence the need for sound preparation. Given that and some organisation (and notes) there is no reason why you cannot find yourself getting to grips with this process quite quickly; indeed, making an initial trade or two can quickly give you confidence and allow you to move on and reach a satisfactory agreement.

The concept of negotiating with variables and specifically of trading them is a core skill in the overall process. You need to:

- Assess all the possible variables ahead of starting a meeting.
- Categorise them and assign them a priority.
- Hold the full list in mind throughout the discussions.
- Trade effectively (optimising and minimising as appropriate).
- Search throughout for possible additional variables.
- Manage the process – repeating and noting agreements and making and using notes as necessary to help you keep track and stay ahead of the game.

However, although this is the core tactic and worth investigating first because of that, a good deal more is involved.

Chapter 4

MAKING IT WORK:
Good tactics, bad tactics and downright ploys

> 'If you have to boil down your negotiating attitude to two things, you can do a lot worse than "question everything" and "think big".'
> *Mark H McComack*

A variety of different techniques must be deployed throughout the negotiation process and this must be done carefully. Indeed, the precise manner in which this is done may make the difference between striking a good deal and merely an OK one. These factors should be regarded as cumulative in effect. One may help; the right mix may clinch the deal. The Duc de la Rochefoucauld once said, "The height of cleverness is to be able to conceal it." This makes the point that the way you deploy such techniques may need to be disguised to some degree.

THE CONDUCT OF THE MEETING
Managing the meeting effectively is important if the complexities are to be coped with and success achieved. During the process two separate factors are in train together: first the process and the tactics of negotiation deployed within it and, secondly, the interpersonal behaviour which goes hand in hand with them. These two factors are both important separately and also in the way that they work together.

In order to build up a clear picture of the process, we will leave the question of interpersonal behaviour to one side until later and deal specifically with the tactical basis for negotiation.

The fundamentals of using variables

To recap what was said earlier about the use of variables, you need to:

- Assess how the variables can be used to trade and also their respective worth.
- Hold variables in mind in order to prepare an opening strategy – a starting point for discussion.
- Assume the possibility that further variables may come into play and continue an ongoing search throughout the negotiation for additional factors that you might use in this way.

We will return to all these points. Meantime, note that occasionally one party in negotiation holds all the cards and the result may be in little doubt. More often the situation is not a foregone conclusion. The balance might go either way and things start apparently on a flat field, but many arrangements are possible. Alongside the core trading, many other techniques of negotiation must be selected and deployed to strengthen what you do and enhance the deal you agree. This chapter reviews what might be called the negotiation armoury. First, we look at what can provide power in negotiating.

SOURCES OF NEGOTIATING POWER

It is the *power* to present a strong case in negotiation that both sides bring to the table and which conditions how well they will do. Everyone hopes to have the balance of power. It is something to consider in your planning and certainly something about which to be realistic; a major mistake made by some negotiators is to over – or under – estimate the power held either by themselves or by the other party.

Negotiators use the word "power" to mean a number of specific things. The main power-generating factors are as follows:

- **Specific variables**: The most obvious sources of power are the specific variables that are most important to a particular negotiation. These can be almost anything, from major matters like financial arrangements including price, discounts and payment terms, to a plethora of others. They can be either tangible or intangible, and usually both are involved. This is an area where feeling is as important as substance. For instance, aspects of the company meeting mentioned earlier may well be subjective: how will the way it is organised affect the participants?

- A **"promise of reward"**: This term describes something you can offer that the other party definitely wants, and acts to ensure that they listen. The banquet manager in the example used earlier wants the business, giving one major element of power to the meeting organiser. There is a corresponding negative side to this which is identified by the next heading.
- A **"threat of punishment"**: This is where there is an apparent intention not to give something that the other party wants. Thus, if the banquet manager refuses to agree some factor important to the organiser, he can wield power; this may be increased if the organiser knows it is short notice and he is unlikely to get availability and a better deal elsewhere.
- **Legitimacy**: Legitimacy means the factual evidence. It can swing the balance without much argument: for example, if the event organiser shows a written quote from another venue then, provided it compares like with like, its presence influences both parties. What is important is that it *seems* to compare like with like; after all, there is a degree of deviousness about negotiation
- **Displaying confidence**: Confidence comes in part from preparation. It has a lot to do with the human and behavioural aspects of negotiation, which are explored in depth later. It is harder to deal with someone who appears very confident (or even quietly confident) and who seems to have every reason to be so. Clearly, you want to feel that the one with the most justifiable confidence is you, and work in every way possible to achieve this
- **Using "bogeys"**: Bogeys are factors used specifically to produce an edge. They may not stand up to great examination, but in the throes of a meeting can be used to good effect. For example, saying, "My director is insistent upon ..." may succeed in labelling a particular point as unalterable so that the truth of the matter

remains hidden and unexplored (and may well be different). Bogies may be factors used only for what they can achieve, or may be factors that are actually of some importance, but which are given artificial weight in the hopes of their securing an advantage.

The precise level of power a negotiator assembles and deploys, and how that is seen by the other party, creates the foundation from which techniques can be deployed and allows the negotiation directed towards your chosen objectives.

When you focus on the bargaining variables in play, try to assess the level of power they give you. This is not simply a numbers game. Having a larger number of variables, while undeniably useful, may not itself guarantee more negotiating power. Some variables may be lightweight and make little difference; others may be particularly telling and add disproportionately to the power you have.

OVERALL GUIDING PRINCIPLES

Here are several core guiding principles which combine to help put your negotiation on a sound footing, see you through the process effectively and which can put you ahead of the game. Remembering and deploying these is perhaps the most important step towards maximising your negotiating expertise. You should:

- Set your sights high.
- Discover the other person's full intentions.
- Hold the entirety of the factors in play in mind.
- Continue looking for further variables throughout the process.

These are so important that they are commented on in turn.

Set your sights high

Always aim high. "Faint heart never won fair lady" goes an old saying and it is important to aim for the top, for the best deal you can imagine; and it is always easier to manage the process from this starting point. If you set your sights high, you can always trade down; indeed you may often have to do so. But it is more difficult to trade up having stated your intentions; indeed doing so may be impossible – the more so the further into the meeting you get. It is for this reason that having a clear view of the variables, the must haves etc. detailed earlier, is so useful. You may not always achieve exactly what you want, but with these approaches the chances of getting close are more likely.

Discovering others' intentions
Other negotiators are not so different from you in what they are doing. They too have a shopping list of what they want to achieve. The better your information about what this is, the better you will be able to operate. Success may relate directly to how much you know about the other person's shopping list; it pays to find out as much as you can.

It is easy to make superficial judgments. There may well be some obvious things they are after, but other factors matter too, as do their priorities. The more complete your picture, the better. Information may come from:

- Prior preparation.
- Knowledge or experience of the person or situation, or ones like them.
- Questions asked as an integral, perhaps early, part of the negotiation meeting.

Infer sensibly by all means, but be wary of making unwarranted assumptions during the meeting as this can lead you on false trails if you are wrong. It is all too easy to come out of a meeting that has not gone so well, saying, "but it seemed so obvious ..." Your thinking so may have been the exact intention of your "adversary". Remember the old saying: "never ass/u/me anything it makes an ass out of you and me".

Hold all the factors in mind
The more we dissect the process, the more the complexities grow. It is easy as you plan ahead to forget some of the issues you need to keep in mind. You need to keep a clear head, to make notes, think and recap as necessary if each step forward is going to be successful.

Find additional variables
Examine every aspect of the meeting as it proceeds to see if there are

additional factors that can be used as variables. You may think of something new, or recognise that factors being assumed or described as fixed can in fact be used, to one degree of another, as variables. It is highly likely that some one will dismiss or gloss over factors precisely so that they are *not* used as variables. So throwaway comments like, "Of course delivery must be by the end of June, other factors need careful consideration, shall we turn to ..." designed to lead you away from a point may need a firm response: "I think there are things to check about delivery; let's take that first –"; one that allows you to revisit the point on your terms.

SMOOTHING THE RIDE

In any kind of negotiation there is always something called the point of balance. It is inherent in the process that while participants start far apart on the scale of possibilities for agreement, they will settle on something they can both relate to as a reasonable deal. The point of balance on which agreement is struck is not, of course, usually spot on the centre of the range of possibilities. A range of solutions is possible around the middle point. Similarly the furthest or most extreme points from the centre are usually quickly recognised by both parties as unrealistic goals and only relevant as starting points, if that. Movement along the scale is what characterises a discussion as negotiating and what moves it towards a position that can be agreed by both parties.

Using what's gone before

There is usually a history of contact between the two negotiating parties – contact does not come out of thin air. This may include written contact, such as correspondence, or earlier meetings. Whether extensive or minimal, such initial communication sets the scene and to some extent provides the agenda. This is often seen in wage bargaining. The employees ask for 8%, the employer snorts with derision and offers 3% and everyone knows that settlement will be somewhere in between (though not necessarily exactly halfway, of course).

Like any other, a negotiation meeting needs an agenda. As part of this it may be useful to recap, to refer to the whole situation so far, to any agreements made or indications given, or to whatever aspect of the history may be useful or necessary. Remember that persuasion proceeds negotiation, so if during first contacts you were concerned with a more fundamental agreement and a case had to be accepted before terms and conditions could be debated, then this too may be worth recapping.

Your first position
The starting point that each party goes for is referred to as the "initial stance". Not least this means starting as you mean to go on – a good start gives you confidence and can wrong foot the other side early on. Care is necessary in choosing your starting point, as the right one can facilitate the moves you want to make thereafter. As examples of the possible options consider:

- **A soft approach**: Towards one end of the scale the conversation might start on a note like, "Let's talk about what you want." Such implies that you are reasonable people and want to secure agreement. This may be more suitable when you do not have such a clearly strong case, but go too far with it and it will create, or increase, the difficulty.
- **The quick kill**: At the other extreme you can go for what is described as the quick kill, "Here are my conditions, take them or leave them." Such an approach does not, in fact, rule out negotiation. It simply starts by making it clear a hard approach is being taken and little will be given away. Working from a powerful position, this or something well to one end may be an appropriate starting point. Such is often used in wage bargaining. But even though it implies strength it must allow for some change or it risks being rejected out of hand. The ritual is important and if people expect some movement this approach may stretch their credibility too much. This, like every other technique, needs using with care.

There is a case for saying that the higher the opening bid (initial stance), the better the final deal achieved by whomever makes it. Certainly it is difficult to negotiate down from nothing and an initially exaggerated stance can pull the other party off balance and change their perception about the kind of deal that might be struck. This can mean that the first phase of negotiation is only a clarification of initial stances. A better, less extreme, point is then adopted by each party. Then negotiation really starts in earnest.

Building bridges

As negotiation begins, on the one hand taking initial stances distances the participants, like two armies taking up positions on opposite hill tops prior to meeting to do battle in the valley between.

Because of this, and because both parties are aware that agreement must involve some movement towards each other's position, there is a need to build what are called "bridges of rapport". These are introduced to bring the parties together or at least closer together in a way that prompts discussion and sets the scene for what needs to be achieved. Each party will introduce bridges that help their own case.

The other party is more likely to see your point of view if they can relate to your position and circumstance. Bridges make this more likely. There are many approaches, for example:

- Begin the discussions on a neutral subject, to allay any hostility, obtain some initial agreement and get the other person talking.
- If you are holding back, give assurance that you will make every effort to come to a mutually agreeable outcome.
- Show respect for both the other party and the process you are embarking on. For example, compliment them about something already done that helps the process.
- Refer back to past agreement. This reinforces persuasion.
- Make clear some of the values in your offering, even if you plan to negotiate them out later.
- Communicate clearly about everything, especially any complex issues.

Tactics such as these put the conversation on a reasonable basis; that is one that seems to others to be reasonable. Even attempts to get the other party's list of requirements on the table can be undertaken in a way that seems helpful: take an interest in them, their needs and views. This combines a show of genuine concern with something that, in fact, adds power and makes your success more likely.

Questioning techniques

Negotiation involves communications in the fullest sense. It is influenced not only by what you say and how you say it, but by what you know about the other party and how you involve them. So, you need to ask questions, and listen – really listen – to the answers. Get the other parties' position clearly in mind. Information is power in negotiation, and while you do not want to make people feel they are undergoing the Spanish Inquisition, the more you aim to discover the better, so your questioning must be made acceptable.

Asking questions may seem sensible enough, but questioning is more than just blurting out the first thing that comes to mind – "why do you say that?"; even a simple phrase may carry overtones and people wonder if you are suggesting they should not have said that, or if you see no relevance for the point made. In addition, many questions can easily be ambiguous. It is all too easy to ask something that, only because it is loosely phrased, prompts an unintended response. Ask, "How long will that take?" and the reply may simply be, "Not long". Ask, "Will you finish that before the meeting scheduled for 11 o'clock on Wednesday?" And, if you asked with that meeting in mind, then you are much more likely to be able to decide exactly what to do when you have a clear answer.

While clarity is important, you also need to consider and use three distinctly different kinds of question:

1. **Closed questions**: these are questions that prompt rapid "Yes" or "No" answers, and are useful both as a starting point (they can also be made easy to answer to help ease someone into the questioning process) and to gain rapid confirmation of something. Too many closed questions on the other hand create a virtual monologue in which the questioner seems to be doing most of the talking and this can be annoying or unsatisfying to the other party.

2. **Open questions**: such questions are phrased so that they *cannot* be answered with a simple "Yes" or "No" and thus they typically begin with words like what, where, why, how, who and when, and phrases such as "Tell me about ..." Such questions get people talking, they involve them and they like the feel they give to a

conversation. By prompting a fuller answer and encouraging people to explain, they also produce far more information than closed questions.

3. **Probing questions**: probing refers to a series of linked questions designed to pursue a point; thus a second question that says, "what else is important about ..." or a phrase like, "Tell me more about ..." get people to go beyond superficial answers and fill out a picture, producing both more detail and exposing the 'why' which lies beyond simpler comments.

Communication can often be made to succeed by the simple prerequisite of starting it with some questions; so too with negotiating. The information you obtain is important. Sometimes you need to keep this close to your chest, but equally you may need to make it clear what you understand and there is power in basing suggestions on their situation – "because you said the urgency was so great it makes sense to ..." The alternative of effectively saying "I suggest", which will be read as saying that this is what you want, is much more likely to be resisted.

Utilising principles such as these really can take negotiating to the next level; working this way will also go a long way to making you seem professional and also towards making your negotiating work effectively and get you the deal you want. But there is more to worry about and the next section reviews further ways to strengthen what you do.

TACTICS TO STRENGTHEN YOUR APPROACH

With the range of core techniques described so far in mind, we now add some additional thoughts by reviewing further techniques that should be in your armoury and that can make your negotiating work well. Consider ten key ideas all of which, separately or together, can act to enhance your basic negotiating skills.

All the following can add strength to what you do. While there is clearly a danger of throwing in every bell and whistle and succeeding only in making matters unmanageable, ignoring such techniques where they will work effectively can risk diluting your success. You need to be prepared to use each or all of the available techniques as appropriate to maximise your negotiating skill. Some orchestration may be necessary here and if you are experimenting maybe it will work best to try adding one or two initially, only adding more when you are managing everything well.

1. The power of silence

Saying nothing can often be as powerful as speaking, providing silence is used at the right time and in the right way. As most people quickly feel embarrassed by a silence, after even a few seconds, it can need a conscious effort to hold it, but it can be worthwhile, to do, for example:

- Being silent can imply certainty on your part, and thus uncertainty in another. Having made a clear suggestion you wait. You will find it's not so difficult to ensure the other person speaks first. Maybe they need to think about it. If you chip in prematurely you may find yourself diluting your case unnecessarily.
- In trading concessions, if you cannot optimise or minimise, silence can imply that you are non-committal.

As an example, imagine: *A company buyer is speaking on the telephone to a potential supplier and, with a good quote in front of him, challenging the price without really saying anything clearly, just, "I am still a bit concerned about the price". The supplier's reflex is to defend the deal as being good, which it is. He asks if it does not seem reasonable to the buyer, who says nothing at all. Embarrassed, the supplier starts to justify the figures and again ends with a question that is ignored. After three silences which the supplier found awkward, he says: "Would another 5% get the order?"* This situation is typical behaviour and so is the outcome – a deal is done! But, from the seller's perspective, it should not be that easy to get a discount. A silence can be powerful. It can be better than asking questions and is always a hard argument to counter. The need to fill the silence can result in your learning more as thoughts are expressed for no better reason than to fill the gap. If your questions are not coped with well by the other party, it is an easy technique with which to win points. Remember the old saying: "Talk less, learn more" – it can add a powerful technique to your negotiating.

2. Reading between the lines

Negotiation is essentially an adversarial process and both parties want the best for themselves, and the only signs of any approaching traps come via the other person, as do signs of success round the corner. You should watch particularly for danger phrases that often mean something other than they seem to, sometimes even the very opposite. For example:

- "It looks like we are about there." Meaning: "There is something else I want."
- "All that's left is to sort out a couple of minor details." Which should prompt the response, "What's that? Minor? For whom?"
- "You're a reasonable fellow." Meaning: "I am."
- "That's much fairer for both of us." Meaning: "Especially for me."
- "That's all, then." Followed by: "But there is just one more thing …"

How carefully you listen is therefore just as important in negotiation as speaking (more of this later). If you read the other person accurately and make it clear that you are so doing, then you can cramp their style negating or diluting possible future ploys and keep the initiative with you.

3. Take notes

The simple fact of jotting down details as you go can help keep complex negotiations on track. While certain meetings are too informal for significant note-taking to be appropriate, even a few words noted down can help. Information is power, especially when you have more pertinent information than the other person.

Be sure you do not leave yourself groping around for what was said. Not only will the lack of recall worry you, but the fact that you are needing to ask calls your expertise into question and may spur the other party on to push harder. Not only will taking notes prevent you being caught out over something factual, but making them or checking them can have another advantage. It gives you time to think. As you say, "Let me just note that down," or as you check, "Let me just see what we agreed about that", you can be thinking. The brain works faster than the pen. It is surprising how much thinking you can do as you write two or three (sometimes irrelevant!) words on your pad. This goes hand in hand with the next point.

4. Summarising frequently

Again this helps with any complexity. As you juggle a number of variables, it is easy to lose the thread. Never be afraid to summarise: recap where you have got to so far and how one aspect of the discussion has been left. Linking this to using the words "suppose" or "if" keeps the conversation organised and allows you to explore possibilities without committing yourself until you are ready. You might make this sort of comment: "Right, you have agreed that you need to sort cost, delivery and timing. Now if you take ...., then ..."

Keep tabs on the exact state of play throughout the process; being organised and on top of things in this way can give you an edge, especially if the other person is less organised than you.

5. Progressively leave people feeling positive

The typical negotiation builds agreement step-by-step. As you proceed make sure you emphasise that each stage is good – preferably in a way that stresses this is so for both parties, but particularly with the emphasis on the other party. Phrases like: "That's a good arrangemen", "That will work well", "That's fair", "That's a good suggestion", help build the agreement. Making people feel that everything is progressing well for them helps maintain a positive, and constructive, feeling to the meeting.

6. Stay neutral

You should maintain neutrality as much and as long as possible. Negotiation works best as a balancing exercise. If you throw the whole basis of discussion up in the air – "None of this is as good as the other deal I am considering" – you risk taking everything back to square one, possibly sufficiently so to make it necessary to switch back to persuasion.

You may want to go back if you are not happy with the offer or the terms and conditions. But if you do, you risk lengthening the whole process; this may be worthwhile, but it could cause problems and an eye must be kept on this. Keeping everything businesslike and professional – using a seemingly dispassionate approach and style – tends to work best in terms of the end result.

7. Play your cards close

Acting too precipitously can be dangerous. Try not to make an offer, certainly not a final offer, until everything that needs negotiating is on the table. This may need no more than a question, "Yes, I am sure I can help there, but is there anything else you want to consider?" You may need to probe to be sure of your ground before you proceed. It is said you should never close off your options until you must; this is good advice in such circumstances.

8. Focus throughout the meeting

Always concentrate. Build in time to think if necessary. The power of silence has been mentioned; use it to think ahead. If necessary use any delaying tactic to stop you getting into difficulty, and always engage the brain before the mouth. Use a calculator, make a telephone call or just say, "Let me think about that for a moment", to give yourself pause for thought. Preparation and practice both make concentration easier, the first because you know what to concentrate on and the second because you learn how important it is to do so. On the other hand, if you can make the other party leap before they look, so much the better.

9. Warning: deadlines

Timing is a variable. How long will things take? When will they happen? All at once? It is said that there has not been a deadline in history that was not negotiable. Keep this in mind at all stages of the process. Remember too that most people build in ample contingency. When someone says something must be done by a particular date, their absolute deadline is almost certainly later.

Remember too that if a deadline is missed, perhaps long after a negotiation has taken place, it will always be noticed and resented. It can make things difficult on future occasions, so action to ensure agreed deadlines are met helps future negotiations.

10. Remembering constraints and variables are interchangeable

Something – everything? – that the other side presents as fixed may be made into a variable. The word fixed is as likely to mean that someone does not *want* to negotiate this, as that they are unwilling or unable to use it as a variable. It pays to act accordingly. As soon as you hear the word "fixed" ask yourself – does it really mean fixed or something else? Very often challenging this will give you a slight edge.

All these tactics are, in themselves, straightforward. They illustrate the multifaceted nature of negotiation, where usually a great deal is going on. Such techniques are useful, but none is a cure-all that will of itself ensure you conclude the deal you want. The trick is in the overall orchestration of what you do. Regard every negotiation meeting as *yours*. Because of the need to orchestrate a complex process, it helps if you are in the driving seat as it were. A line in Shakespeare's *Much Ado About Nothing* puts it well, saying that if: "Two men ride of a horse, one must ride behind."

Meetings, too, need someone in front, taking the lead. Taking a leading role does not have to mean wielding an obviously heavy hand; indeed, it may not even be obvious from where direction originates. Run the conversation that *you* want, in a way that *they* find they like, or at least find acceptable or professional, and you will do better at keeping the meeting on track in the way you want. So beware: it is all too easy for the reverse to happen and for you to find you are being led by the nose.

If you make sure to get off to a good start it sets the process in train. Finetuning as you go along keeps you progressing matters as you want, towards your goals and along the lines of your plan. This means you being extra conscious of what the other person appears to be up to and of how the interpersonal behaviour of the transaction (a topic we review in the next chapter) is likely to work.

A TEAM APPROACH

There are many techniques to consider individually and the entirety of the process is important too. Matters may be complex and any meeting may consist of a lengthy discussion, especially if several people are involved.

If you are part of a team, albeit only two of you, it is essential to discuss the matter ahead of the meeting and lay out a strategy. To avoid tripping over each other as it were, you must agree and arrange a logical order for the discussion and consider how to work together. A team must divide the tasks between them – if two people are involved then one will lead on some points, another on others, but someone must be in overall charge. This is primarily to keep things manageable.

Though it is important for everyone to be involved in the discussion, one may well have the smaller proportion of the tasks. Such a person is the obvious choice to keep notes and monitor the developing balance. Having the best view of how things stand at any particular moment, such a person will be responsible for keeping the two of them (or more) on track during discussions, which will inevitably get more confusing as they progress.

The thinking described above makes good sense. Maintaining a vision of the broad picture as you proceed is as important as the tactics deployed at a particular moment to settle an issue. Note that when more than one person on each side is involved in discussions, how the team organises itself becomes a variable and a key factor in securing an edge. In good teamwork, one and one makes more than two. The way people work together should appear seamless, and can add considerable strength to a situation if this is deployed as an active ingredient and made to work well.

Overall, the key issues of the process at this stage can be summarised by noting that you should always:

- Be sure you know what gives you (and them) power.
- Act to keep the process manageable: focus on the key operational process of negotiation, such as setting your sights high.
- Prepare carefully, not least so that you are able to make a good start.

- Handle the trading process that forms the core of negotiation effectively.
- Understand the techniques, and when and how they are best deployed.

There are many skills that demand a considerable breadth of thinking. The mind must seemingly focus on an impossible span of disparate things and do so in a way that allows something to be done right. How do people (well some people) manage to juggle with flaming torches without burning holes in the carpet? But they do, even if the fire department were called out a few times before they got the hang of it. The danger here is that as you begin to face the range of things that need doing in something like negotiating, everything becomes overwhelming.

However, you should not despair – practice makes perfect. Things do come together and the trick in making that happen is simply not to bite off more than you can chew. If you think about what you want to do, introduce techniques progressively and allow habits to form that will make the process easier, then it is possible.

It then perhaps easy to imagine putting all the factors mentioned so far to work, at least in theory, but you are not alone – it is not like making an uninterrupted presentation. The people you negotiate with and how they behave do not make it easy. Understanding the behavioural element in negotiation helps you deal with this and decide how you should act too.

Chapter 5

THE INTERPERSONAL ELEMENT
The behavioural interactions

> 'Whatever else you are doing ... it is worth asking yourself,
> "Am I paying enough attention to the people problem?"'
> *Roger Fisher*

There is no negotiation without people and the way that participants in negotiation behave, albeit with some of what goes on being intangible, colours, indeed influences, every negotiation meeting – and its outcome. An eye must be kept on this too, watching what is being done to you and deploying certain behaviour in aid of your own intentions. This chapter sets out the key issues that you need in mind to operate successfully on this level and thus put together a strong overall approach.

Beyond the techniques, negotiation also depends on reading the behaviour of the other people involved, and using behavioural factors yourself. Reading between the lines and acting accordingly is part of the negotiating ritual. To a degree, fluency in this is a matter of experience, which needs time to accumulate. Nevertheless, certain principles can be useful. Next we look in turn at the key behavioural aspects of negotiation, everything from reading between the lines to non-verbal signals.

HIDDEN SIGNALS

There is a language peculiar to negotiation. Some of what is said becomes ritual; it is clearly part of the fabric rather than the content of what is being done. Some is a ploy, effectively an attempt to deceive and create a unfair advantage if the other party is unwary. And thus it is sometimes necessary to read between the lines to see what motivation lies behind what is actually said.

Certain general classic phrases are familiar to us as things that raise a question; our instinct tells us that they should not be believed. These include, "Trust me. I only say this for your own good" and "The cheque is in the post". Here the complexities are greater and it is hidden meanings we are after. Consider the hidden signals in the following examples shown with a suggested undertone in brackets:

- "My organisation would find it extremely difficult to meet the deadline." (*If we do meet it, it must be worth something.*)
- "We are just not set-up to cope with that." (*So if we do, consider it a significant favour.*)
- "I do not have the authority to arrange ..." (*... but someone else has.*)
- "Let's discuss that point." (*It is negotiable.*)
- It is not our normal practice to do that (*But I could make an exception.*)
- "The price is fixed and cannot be negotiated." (*If you want to – you start.*)
- "Our policy doesn't permit me to give additional discounts and if it did they would not be as much as 10%. (*Would you accept 5%?*)
- "Our price for that quantity is X" (*But for larger quantities ...*)
- "We are not prepared to discuss that at this stage." (*But we will later.*)
- "That's very much more than our budget." (*So it had better add real value and extra benefits.*)
- "Well, I can't say I am happy with the arrangement but ..." (*I agree that, but may ask for something else to balance it.*)
- "That's the standard terms and conditions." (*And I hope I don't have to vary them, but I will if I must.*)
- "It seems an extremely reasonable arrangement." (*It is best for me.*)

- "This is a good price." (*It's profitable for us*.)

There are doubtless more you can spot, and may use in future – many more. The detail, the nuances of everything said when negotiating is very important. Does what is said mean exactly what it seems? Can you check? Is it a ploy? Does it present an opportunity? How can you gain an edge with a word or phrase? Keep your ears open and be vigilant; it is wise to be constantly watchful, to take nothing at face value, at least initially.

Remember that while you use phrases with nuances they help you, if the other party uses similar things they may provide warning signs, or potentially take you in a direction that puts you at a disadvantage. Recognising them, and their potential danger, is the first step to overcoming them if it is you that they are deployed against.

BEHAVIOURAL INFLUENCES

There are almost limitless behavioural factors that can play a part in negotiation discussions. The following are typical and illustrate the range.

Controlling "the temperature"

Sometimes circumstances mean that the conversation can easily become heated, on either side. But you negotiate best with a calm, considered approach. While you do not want to make it easy for the other person, you do not want the fabric of a negotiation to collapse either. Any behaviour you use must help your cause without undermining the process.

Sometimes by pursuing your cause you can end up doing more harm than good. For instance, if you labour an issue on which agreement is difficult and refuse to budge, particularly early on in a discussion, you may create an impasse from which it is difficult for either party to retreat. You need to keep the range of issues in mind. If one point is causing problems, common ground cannot be found and things are in danger of getting heated, then you might leave that point on one side to return to later. Having agreed some of the issues, overall views change and revisiting something may result in (sometimes easy) agreement. At a later stage with a deal now near, an early sticking point may not seem so important and can then be dealt with without real difficulty.

Beware icebergs

The danger to shipping of icebergs is not so much because of what can be seen of them, but because most of their volume cannot be seen; it is hidden below the surface. The iceberg concept can apply to discussion and negotiation. You ask something and do not seem to get a straight answer. The other party's suspicion may prevent it – they are so busy looking for hidden motives that they hinder agreement for no good reason. It makes sense to spell out why you are doing things, asking a certain question, "If you can tell me ... then I ...", pursuing a certain line so that at least most of what is hidden becomes clear.

Of course, you may have motives it is better to keep hidden, at least for the moment, but it will not help if the other person thinks your level of deviousness is way above what it actually is.

Signing the way

Signposting (or flagging) as it is called is the spelling out of how you are proceeding; it can help clarity, understanding and assist progress. Sometimes it just makes clear what you are doing: "May I ask ...?" Or "Perhaps I might suggest ...?" At other times a specific reason makes getting what you want more likely: "I think it might be easier to settle other details if you can agree a fixed budget first." This can be seen as a constructive step forward. On the other hand, you should never flag disagreement. This is something to watch, as the natural response is to flag it instantly. Consider what happens in a simple example, one showing how listening is affected:

Imagine John makes a suggestion: "Perhaps you can aim for completion of stage one by Friday week." Mary immediately disagrees: "No, I think that's far too long." Even if they go on to explain why, and even if they are right, John is busy developing a retaliatory response from the moment he hears the word "no". John does not listen to the explanation of why, and even if it is half-heard, he is already committed to a riposte. When reasons are given before disagreement is flagged, people are more likely to listen constructively – and more likely to accept the reasons given.

It follows that, if John makes the same point Mary could respond in a way that initially seems to agree, "That would be ideal. However, you agreed that the whole project should be finished by the end of the month. Does Friday week leave sufficient time for everything else?" Alternatively, John might precede his suggestion with a reason. In either case there is much more chance that this will prompt thought and discussion, and thus that a counter-suggestion will be accepted or a compromise found.

Regular summary

The act of summarising regularly always helps the process, particularly as many negotiations get complex and discussions can last a while. Here doing so will:

- Help you gain the initiative in the discussion, or maintain the dialogue.
- Check progress and allow you to rephrase things said by the other party.
- Make sure that both parties have similar interpretations of what is said, and thus avoid misunderstanding and subsequent acrimony.

The fact of regular summarising will not only help keep the discussion on track, but if you adopt the role of doing it (something that may merely be regarded as helpful) then it will also help put you in the driving seat and influence your profile.

Psychological attack

Certain things are said, not as a tangible part of any argument, but to put the other party at a psychological disadvantage – to rattle them. Such comments may be based on issues which are part of the discussion, such as pressure on timing and deadlines. Others may be solely cosmetic, like a (contrived) interruption – a pause to make an urgent telephone call, for instance. Such ploys create a long silence or pause in the discussion, during which the instigator can be thinking and you are sweating. All sorts of things can be used in this way, some examples follow:

- **What appears to be total fluency with the facts**: wondrous mental arithmetic may have been worked out beforehand, or it

could be just be a guess, one said with sufficient authority to sound definitive.
- **Physical arrangements**: an uncomfortable chair or position, balancing a coffee cup and trying to take notes.
- **Playing for time**: working something out on a calculator or making a phone call.
- **Injecting irrelevant digression**.
- **A smoke screen of demands**, only one of which is important.
- **Flattery or coercion**.
- **Angry outburst** or a show of emotion.
- **Pretended there is misunderstanding**.
- **Financial restraints** made to seem irreversible.

This is a list to which you might add; it is also an area where, if you must negotiate regularly with someone, it pays to learn their style.

Defend/attack spirals

People often feel it is not proper to hit someone without warning, and thus disagreement often starts from mild beginnings. When one person says they are not sure about something, or that they think they should aim for something better, this begins to gently move them towards a major negative; by acting this way, you allow the other person to sense what is happening and begin to prepare a counter-argument.

A better tactic is not to put someone on their guard, thus effectively providing time for them to react well. If it is appropriate to attack, then good negotiators do so firmly, at once and without warning. The response this prompts may likely be easier to deal with.

Making counter suggestions

Imagine that you make proposal X and then the other person makes proposal Y. If you automatically think they are disagreeing, you will not be receptive and may not consider the alternative properly. If so, your riposte can lead into a series of monologues, with both sides seeing the other as unhelpful and unconstructive. Progress is blocked, perhaps even when proposal X and Y are not really so far apart and things could be moving together. Avoiding this danger needs careful reading of what is being said.

Avoiding deadlock

Your aim in negotiating is to make a deal. Deadlock does nothing for either party. The search for variables has to go on until a mutually acceptable deal is possible. It is usually only a question of time. However, if there are moments of deadlock it is helpful to think of the conversation flowing like a stream, which will always find a path round obstructions rather than through them.

You should never underestimate the chances of a new path, nor over-estimate your opponent's power and determination to remain unmoving. Try to find out why there is deadlock, and search widely for concessions or variables that will break it. In dire cases suggest a break, agreeing as much as possible before it, or even adding in the involvement of other people. Try anything to create a real shift in what is happening and move matters closer to your own goal.

The ritual, and how to use it

If you visit say Singapore (or many other countries for that matter) you will find that it is necessary to bargain in the shops and markets, not simply to secure a good price but to win respect. The process itself is important, not just the outcome. So it is too for any negotiating situation. Some professional negotiators, who enjoy the game, feel frustrated if agreement is too quick or too simple. Certainly negotiation must be allowed to take its course, and some people will put up more and more conditions or elements to keep the process going. In such circumstances it may be wise never to make the first offer, and not to drive impossible bargains or lay down unacceptable conditions.

An international example makes a point also about different situations demanding different approaches. *A man is visiting Hong Kong for the first time and wishes to buy a watch. He had been told about the bargaining and the percentage drop in price for which he should aim. He sets off round the shops and, despite his best efforts, only gets halfway towards the suggested discount. Back at the hotel, discussing this with a local colleague, he asked what it was he was doing wrong. "How long were you in each shop?" asked the colleague. On hearing that it was ten minutes or so, he suggested the visitor try again and give it 20/30 minutes. The newcomer then discovered that only after 20 or so, when you're sitting on a stool and coffee has been produced, did the bargaining get serious. Next time he came out with a nice watch and a good deal, and a little more understanding about the psychology of negotiation and the way things work in this different culture.*

Of course there are limits, but if the other party wants to take their time, let them. It may be worthwhile in the end. Timing is an important factor and has to be handled just right (you can get into trouble if you are in effect a time-waster). Do not underestimate what is going on at a psychological level – doing so can put you at serious disadvantage and even one such seemingly small thing can see the deal you finally settle for weakened.

An eye on the future

You should always aim to end on a pleasant note. Negotiation can get acrimonious, hard bargains are driven, but people may well need to work together again. It may be good for future relations for the last move to be towards the other party, maybe throwing in one last small sweetener as the final agreement is made. This can stand you in good stead next time round. Negotiating with colleagues may be a regular part of your work and you do not want one resounding win to make every future exchange more difficult.

It pays to keep potential future dealings and relationships in mind at every stage of the negotiation process.

THE POWER OF LISTENING

Failure to listen, or at least to listen carefully, is at the heart of many a communication problem. It is always important, especially in a complex interaction such as negotiation. It is easy to be distracted, and you need to concentrate. Letting your thoughts digress, however constructively, is all too easy. Give the other party your undivided attention and you put yourself in place to negotiate powerfully.

Emotion adds another distraction. While the other person's argument unfolds you perhaps begin to feel anxious, or become angry; and if such resentment takes over and prevents you listening, your case will suffer. You may want to keep your first reactions hidden and it can be difficult to refer back, saying that something is a minor difficulty, if when it was raised total dismay was what showed, all too obviously, on your face.

Clarify if necessary
Although it can seem awkward, never be afraid to interrupt a long speech to double-check you are following it. The penalties of letting the conversation run on with you being unclear on some (possibly key) issue are likely to be severe. This outweighs any awkwardness about interrupting. Just ask for simplification or repetition if you wish; people are unlikely to find real fault with this as they want you to understand their argument. Beware too of hearing what you want to hear. Do not make assumptions, act only on what the true message is. You may need to analyse the message as it proceeds and begin to form a response, but you have to keep listening as you do so if you are not to run into problems. Remember that one missed point may not only cause a momentary hiatus, but – undiscovered – it might also have you labouring under a misapprehension throughout an entire conversation.

Making listening easier
It makes sense to also think about what will make listening easier. You cannot concentrate on what is being said if there is a lot of background noise in, for example, an open-plan office, or if you are busy with something else as you talk, like sorting documents. Try to pick a time when you are at your best, not over-tired or distracted by some personal emergency. The checklist that follows (which is adapted from the companion volume in this *Smart Skills Series*, *Persuasion* by Patrick Forsyth) shows how you can maximise the effectiveness of your listening.

Before we get to that, however, pause for a moment here and, without looking back, ask yourself if you can remember the four words in the main heading leading into the topic of listening? If not (and be honest) then consider that the principle her is similar. Without concentration we do not take in every detail of what we are reading or hearing – even in an important meeting.

It is important therefore to regard listening as an *active* process. It is something we all need to work at. What does this mean? There is what is a perhaps surprising amount of ways in which we can focus and improve our listening – and the retention of information heard, including the details crucial to understanding that doing so enables.

These include the need to:

- **Appear like a good listener**: people will appreciate it, and if they see they have your attention and feedback will be more forthcoming.
- **Want to listen**: this is easy once you realise how useful it is to the communication process.
- **Understand**: it is not just the words but the meaning that lies behind them you must note.
- **React**: let people see that you have heard, understood and are interested. Nods, small gestures, signs and comments will encourage the other person's confidence and participation – right?
- **Stop talking**: other than small acknowledgements, you cannot talk and listen at the same time. Do not interrupt.
- **Use empathy**: put yourself in the other person's shoes and make sure you really appreciate their point of view.
- **Check**: if necessary, ask questions promptly to clarify matters as the conversation proceeds. An understanding based even partly on guesses or assumptions is dangerous. But ask questions diplomatically; avoid saying, "You didn't explain that properly".
- **Remain unemotional**: too much thinking ahead – "However can I overcome that point?" – can distract you.
- **Concentrate**: allow nothing to distract you.
- **Look at the other person**: nothing is read more rapidly as disinterest than an inadequate focus of attention – good eye contact is essential (and furthermore, in negotiating a lack of it will always be read as deviousness).
- **Note particularly key points**: edit what you hear so that you can better retain key points manageably.
- **Avoid personalities**: do not let your view of someone as a person distract you from the message, or from dealing with them if that is necessary.
- **Do not lose yourself in subsequent arguments**: some thinking ahead may be useful; too much and you may suddenly find you have missed something.
- **Avoid negatives**: to begin with clear signs of disagreement (even a dismissive look) can make the other person clam up and destroy the dialogue.
- **Make notes**: do not trust your memory, and if it is polite to do so, ask permission before writing their comments down.

All this may seem obvious, but if you listen – really listen – then everything that follows will be a little easier and more certain. If you pick up 100% of the message, you are in a much better position to respond effectively. Remember the old saying that "there is a good reason why we find ourselves with two ears and one mouth". Listening is certainly worth some thought.

ASKING QUESTIONS
Never get too far into negotiations without asking sufficient questions to help you with the whole process. Ask about the other person, their situation, their needs, and their priorities. You may find you have some questions that regularly need asking, for example:

- "Shall we aim to finish by ...?"
- "Do other people need to be involved in these arrangements?"
- "Do you have a firm budget for this?"
- "What's actually most important to you here?"

Beyond this, of course, particular situations lead to specific questions.

As has been said, open questions, that is those which cannot be answered simply yes or no and tend to start with the words what, where, why, how, who, are usually best. They get people talking and produce more information. This is the raw material for your case. The question of questioning was investigated earlier (see page 59) and will not be repeated here.

Remember: finding a black cat in a dark coal cellar is difficult until it scratches you. Similarly, it is difficult to negotiate if there are too many gaps in your knowledge about the situation. You may just find yourself boxed into a corner. If in doubt ...ask and ask at once; if you let the moment pass, it may be impossible to check later without appearing weak. And you don't want to find yourself agreeing to a less than ideal arrangement as you say to yourself: "If only I had asked ..."

BODY LANGUAGE
Reading between the lines of what is said is important, but words, tone and emphasis are not the only ways messages come over when you speak with someone. People project all sorts of non-verbal clues to their

feelings. Some of these are routine: a nod intended to mean "yes", a grunt obviously expressing derision. We normally take these in our stride, though in negotiation they must not be missed.

Body language may be an inexact science, but it is interesting and perhaps worth some study (the greatest "expert" on the subject is Allan Pease who has written several books on the topic). A single gesture is not an infallible sign of anything. An unbuttoned jacket (which supposedly indicates open-mindedness) may only mean it is a tight fit; wearing a jacket at all may indicate fierce air conditioning rather than formality.

Your intention should be not to over-react to anything, or to use one gesture as an infallible sign, but you must not ignore indications that could be useful either. Proceed with care and keep an eye on body language through the whole process of negotiation; remember, though, body language can only provide clues and it should not become a fixation; although if overwhelming signs match in with what is being said then such indications are likely to be accurate.

Let's go overseas for an example: *a meeting is about to take place in Singapore. A European visitor has had some correspondence with the general manager of a local organisation and a meeting is arranged. The European is greeted cordially, offered a drink and as the meeting seems about to get underway he is given a business card. He tucks it quickly in his top pocket and begins to state his case.*

This may seem to be a small point, but the ritual of business card exchange is an important one in the East. It is expected that you study a card, give it a moment, view it as important and store it safely. Certainly you need to hand over one of your own in exchange. Not doing so will not make the discussion collapse in ruins, but failure to understand local conditions might have a (small) negative effect that weighs in the balance.

What's the moral? It pays to check the particulars of behaviour and social nuance. It is one thing to check currency rates and tariffs, it is another to remember not to point your feet at someone in case it causes offence, as in Buddhist countries. This example makes a general point which may stand further investigation if you plan to deal internationally and must work in and understand a specific local culture. In fact, a more general situation may apply with any individual where particular circumstances rein (this may just mean an engineer, an IT specialist or whatever; all have their own ways).

The reason for being sensitive to what is said, nuances, gestures and so on, is to help you stay in line with the two basic factors of negotiation: your plan and your reading of how things are going and being received throughout the meeting.

TACTICAL RESPONSES

Certain ploys occur often enough to have collected names. The examples set out here may help accelerate your experience. They indicate some of the tactics you may face (each is described as a range) and suggest both what the other party hopes for as a result and what your possible response might be.

- *Not me* – *claims they cannot make a decision, must refer to boss, committee or whoever.*
  Hoping you will: yield to pressure without souring relations, while they say, "It is not my fault".
  Your action: ask questions to ascertain whether it is true or just a ploy. In some meetings it may be worth checking early on whether they have the authority to make an arrangement.

- *The only option* – *keeps suggesting unacceptable option, without alternative.*
  Hoping you will: be forced into agreement, seeing no other option.
  Your action: keep calm, bear your objectives firmly in mind, suggest other alternatives such as a middle ground, and keep restating the problem.

- *No way* – *immediately stating one element as non-negotiable.*
  Hoping you will: give up or offer a great deal to try to make it negotiable.
  Your action: offer to set that element aside, moving on to other things and getting back to it once rapport is established and agreement is clear on some other elements.

- ***What?*** – *overreaction to something, shock-horror to indicate an impasse.*
  <u>Hoping you will</u>: offer a rapid concession to compensate.
  <u>Your action</u>: ignore the first response and restate the issue to prompt a more considered, informative response.

- ***Chaos*** – *displays anger, storms out, takes umbrage.*
  <u>Hoping you will</u>: apologise, give concession, or get angry (and thus more vulnerable) yourself.
  <u>Your action</u>: keep calm, express your concern at any misunderstanding, seek clarification, and let things return to normal before trying to proceed.

- ***Poor me*** – *plea for special sympathy, concern or approach because of their situation.*
  <u>Hoping you will</u>: give more away because you feel sorry for them.
  <u>Your action</u>: do not be put off or be overly sympathetic, acknowledge the problem, restate your position and take the conversation back on track.

- ***Can't because ...*** – *opens with an initial, intractable problem: "You can't do anything unless the project can be completed by the end of the month."*
  <u>Hoping you will</u>: concede
  <u>Your action</u>: ask questions to discover the truth; it is likely such an initial stance is a ploy or smokescreen.

- ***No-can-do*** – *contains no detail or reason but is very negative: "That's just not at all acceptable."*
  <u>Hoping you will</u>: see a point as intractable and give in.
  <u>Your action</u>: ask for detail, why is it unacceptable? How different does it need to be to be acceptable? Get away from the unspecific and down to the facts.

- ***Something extra*** – *an overt request for some extra benefit.*
  <u>Hoping you will</u>: give it to gain goodwill and keep things going.

<u>Your action</u>: investigate the trading possibilities. If I give you X, would you be able to agree to Y?

- **Policy** – *the rules are quoted: "More than my job's worth" (for example company policy).*
  <u>Hoping you will</u>: read it as unchangeable and not even try to negotiate.
  <u>Your action</u>: check whether it is true, whether there are exceptions or others have authority to make them. Rules are made to be broken but be prepared for this to be difficult on occasion and, if necessary, to leave it.

- **Persuade me** – *negotiation is dependent on a tacit agreement, e.g. to buy or take action. If the deal is put into question, the whole situation may be changing.*
  <u>Hoping you will</u>: give in to secure agreement.
  <u>Your action</u>: ask questions, do you go back to the stage of persuasion, find out if it is a ploy? If so, stick to your position and push back hard.

- **Large versus small** – *a big deal is made of a small point, and then used as a concession for something they really want.*
  <u>Hoping you will</u>: see the first as a real issue and trade in a way that is not a good exchange.
  <u>Your action</u>: check real importance, compare and deal with the two things together.

- **No progress** – *things appear to be deadlocked, no clear way out.*
  <u>Hoping you will</u>: give in as only way forward.
  <u>Your action</u>: suggest a real change, a break, an arbitrator. If it is a ploy, these may be resisted and you can get back on track.

It may be worth keeping notes of your own examples of such things, as an aide memoir for the future and your future planning. In every case the trick with this sort of thing is not to be phased, think clearly and seek a logical way ahead.

TOWARDS SUCCESS

Negotiation involves a number of aspects. The process itself is important, the structure and sequence of events also contribute to its success. The ritual may be important too, the techniques certainly are, but it is ultimately people that make it work, so no aspect of interpersonal behaviour must be overlooked or underestimated.

Difficulties are likely to be less because the individual elements are themselves complex, occurring rather because of the problem of orchestrating the whole thing and missing details. The power of interpersonal behaviour in negotiating is just one element that can make success more likely. You can usefully ask:

- How can you use behavioural factors to avoid dangers that are created for you in negotiation?
- Similarly, how can you spot opportunities to increase your power and influence in negotiation using such tactics?
- What particular factors do you think you can identify and use that play to your style and strengths?

It is those who get every aspect of the process moving together as a co-ordinated whole who are likely to make the best and most effective negotiators. So, you must:

- Concentrate throughout any negotiation meeting. There will always be a great deal to take in
- Remain alert throughout for any sign, any nuance that might assist you in the process, and be ready to finetune what you do
- Remember that behavioural factors can give warning of dangers, allowing you to take action to avoid them, and highlight opportunities, allowing you to strengthen the effectiveness of your tactics.

The very nature of the process means that constant finetuning is necessary as you go. Just as in a sailing boat a hand needs to be kept on the tiller to compensate for wind and tide and maintain smooth progress towards a destination, so it is with negotiation. However well-planned your tactics, you are constantly having to respond to what the other party does. Sometimes this means dealing with something you expected, at least at some point and in some form, and which you can therefore be prepared for. On other occasions it means responding quickly to something surprising.

A DASH OF CREATIVITY

Sometimes it also means taking a creative approach, sometimes one with inherent risk. An idea that changes – perhaps radically – your position and/or profile in the negotiation and improves your chances of success may well be worth trying. Ideas here can clearly go too far and, as was said, may involve an element of risk, but such approaches are worth thinking about. The two examples shown illustrate the kind of thing hinted at here:

- *It is said that an advertising agency that was negotiating with British Railways (BR) about a campaign to promote the Pullman (refreshment) services on trains kept the BR team waiting a long time in their Reception. The area was noisy, untidy and after they began to be impatient some indifferent tea and coffee were served in paper cups, on a dirty tray swimming in coffee dregs and biscuit crumbs. Finally, when they were on the point of walking out, the team were shown into the conference room and in welcoming them the agency man explained that they had just seen how their passengers saw the existing service on their trains and that they would help them put this right. A risky strategy no doubt (though reputed to have worked) and – true or not – the story illustrates a creative approach; one can certainly imagine that the agency team would be seen in a good light for their novel approach (provided the ideas they then put forward were good).*

- *In a the smart European office of a company making ball bearings, a consultant is negotiating with management about a training contract. As he arrived in Reception he was given a visitors' pass, stamped with his name and time of arrival. On leaving, the card was replaced with one recording the impressive number of ball bearings made in the factory during the duration of his visit. Rather than keeping it he asked for an envelope and sent it back to the manager in the marketing department with whom he had been in discussions with a copy of his business card attached. On their card, below the word "produced", he wrote a short phrase: "...but how many have you sold?" Again, there was a risk involved here, the manager might have thought it impolite, but in fact, following a meeting about training intended to improve sales results, it made precisely the right impression – the terms of the deal were agreed without further discussion.*

Both these examples act to change positively the image and, therefore, in terms of negotiations, the power of the people concerned. Ideas of this sort can be an important part of establishing the relationship inherent in negotiating and are worth some thought – along with some careful judgement.

Whatever techniques and tactic are used, the overall objective is to remain on course, and however good your planning may be negotiation is a dynamic process and one where realistically not everything will work out just as you anticipate or want; some give and take and some finetuning along the way is always necessary. Some of this can only come with practice. It is always worth analysing what went well, what went less well and what there is to learn from a negotiation, whatever the outcome.

Given this approach, the number of proven tactics in your armoury can only increase and with them your ability to be a successful negotiator. All that relates to the interpersonal behaviour issues is no exception.

Chapter 6

THE FINE PRINT
The contractual elements of a deal

> 'The big print giveth and the fine print taketh away.'
> *J Fulton Sheen*

A handshake may well seal a deal. But more may be necessary and the circumstances of some negotiations may need much more, with the old phrase about "crossing Ts and dotting Is" hardly doing justice to the formality involved and the need to tie down every detail. Indeed, the need for formality is perhaps increasing; consider the trends affecting most of us in the workplace.

THE NEW REALITIES

All the main trends affecting businesses and organisations over recent years (and not so recent, for that matter) affect the likely need for, and importance of, negotiation. In current circumstances, people will not settle for an arrangement without consideration and often without seeking to better it. The main factors affecting this attitude are as follows:

- **Financial pressures**: taxation, interest rates, more pressure on cashflow and more pressure from shareholders, banks and any other stakeholder involved (including staff who always want a greater slice of the pie; though equally these days they may be concerned for their jobs). All highlight any situation that affects the key financial ratios. Thus, for example, people more fiercely seek to protect margins in negotiations with suppliers and, to take a wholly different example, a harder line is taken with union demands. Recently, the financial pressures have been extreme and this situation looks unlikely to change any time soon.

- **Administrative burdens**: largely, so the conventional wisdom has it, government inspired. Whatever the truth of that, paperwork – from matters linked to everything from employment law to the provision of information and compliance with edicts of all sorts – does take up significant time; and as yet the long-awaited "paperless office" is nowhere in sight. Anything threatening to increase this burden is resisted. This might mean negotiating with a supplier simply to create a smoother administrative process between supplier and supplied, or again, negotiations designed to make or save money in light of what is perceived as being spent on (perhaps unnecessary) administration.
- **Competition**: market conditions seem to get more and more competitive; and international competition is a major factor in this picture. This in turn increases risk, reduces margins and creates an attitude that anywhere that might produce (or save) money must be pursued hard.
- **Technology**: of all sorts, and information technology in particular, is a wonder of the age. There is no doubt that it brings major efficiency and convenience; but it also brings cost, a steep learning curve and an apparently built-in obsolescence that means many people feel they are on a technological rollercoaster and there is always something new to get to grips with. Again, although it can be a route to financial savings, costs are perceived as growing and financial criteria assume greater priorities.

In fact all the trends and processes affecting business can have implications that lead to more hard-nosed attitudes about money and tougher negotiations. Environmental factors are now more important too, and more costly. Government restrictions also tend to prompt higher costs (e.g. complying with more stringent safety regulations). Beyond all this, attitudes change – many of those working in an organisation are so used to the concept of getting a good deal, questioning what is offered and negotiating that it has become an automatic reflex. It may occur in one area for good practical reasons, and those who must exercise negotiating skills in one situation, deploy them wherever else possible. After all, the fact that praise is collected for a good deal done easily tends to keep the trend for more negotiation going.

New realities in the marketplace

So many markets have had economic difficulties, if not outright recession, in recent years that this has inevitably had an effect on the attitudes and therefore on the practices of all those affected by them. As one prime application of negotiation is linked to sales, this makes a good example. In recent years buyers are likely to:

- Use a greater number of suppliers (perhaps playing them off against each other).
- Be better informed and to check more details in advance of discussions.
- Want to take less risk.
- Be more demanding (of service, quality and whatever they describe as "value for money").
- Think, and make decisions, on a shorter-term basis.
- Delay decisions (or simply not buy for a period – "replacing the company cars can be held over until next year").
- Reduce stock levels held.
- Want more formal arrangements – "put it in writing" – and agreed terms valid for longer.
- Be less loyal to suppliers.
- Want longer credit terms, pay later regardless – or both.

You might well add to this list; certainly an overall increased toughness is likely to be in evidence in a number of ways; including things where detailed negotiations are now necessary, when in the past a reasonable package might have been accepted without question.

Whatever the specifics involved here, a new breed of buyer has evolved, all of whom – whatever their own individual reasons – make much tougher negotiating adversaries.

THE POWER OF MAJOR ACCOUNTS

One specific category of buyers worth an individual mention is those within key or major accounts. The relevant point here is one of power. In so many industries the share of markets is spread across fewer and fewer potential customers; in fast-moving consumer goods (FMCG), product manufacturers in many countries find that there are only four or five major suppliers with perhaps 80% of the market or more between them. The need to sell to them is high: lose one and a major part of the market is lost. They thus wield considerable power. They are in a strong position to secure the deal they want and a long list of variables needs to be thrashed out with them before a deal can be struck; and all of these concern cost and reflect directly on profitability. The list below sets out some examples and may ring bells even if you are not in the FMCG area.

Powerful major customers

The kinds of thing – all variables – that a manufacturer might be pressed on by a major customer include:

- Additional time from the field sales force (for instance, to help merchandising).
- Discounts (and there may be many different reasons for them, e.g. quantity bought or when purchase is made; and some are retrospective).
- Any special packaging and packing.
- Delivery (maybe to multiple locations).
- Special labelling.
- Returns and damage arrangements.
- Advertising and promotional support, including financial contributions.
- Merchandising materials.
- Training of customers' staff.
- Financing (including special credit terms).

These sorts of cost are, of course, all in addition to normal production and distribution costs. Yet major players can make demands here that quickly put margins under pressure, knowing that the pressure for the supplier to maintain a relationship with them is intense.

On the other side, a buyer – say a retailer – does not want to alienate a supplier and miss the opportunity of profiting from selling a good product. So, realistically, a balance is necessary; it is however one that the supplier may sometimes think is tending to be rather one-sided. Whatever else, in most developed markets, it dictates that negotiation takes place.

WHY CONTRACTS ARE NECESSARY

While sometimes negotiations, however hard fought, are essentially informal – people know each other well, the matter is regarded as straightforward and transient, no elaborate record is necessary and both parties are content to implement whatever has been agreed – often the reverse is true.

Similarly, in terms of contractual arrangement: all negotiations may need to state clear arrangements, but sometimes it is felt nothing needs to be put in writing. It should, though, be noted that a verbal contract can be binding in a Court of Law (and so too can an email). Consider very carefully what you regard as informal. Make sure that nothing formal is in fact necessary. Formalities are less necessary when all goes well, in which case goodwill will see things through. But they exist to catch situations that change or cannot be foreseen. Such things might include, for example, a change of personnel in a company. It is clearly a problem if the person with whom you make a clear, but informal, arrangement is suddenly no longer there when a problem occurs; the problem will be worse if the new person is not only ignorant of the arrangement, but antagonistic to it.

As the trends with which we started this chapter make clear, with other negotiations the arrangements do need documenting; perhaps "must be" is a better way of putting it. Often the setting out of terms and conditions, or other arrangements, is intended to be formal, contractual and is very necessary. Once agreed the parties are stuck with them. No review of negotiating would therefore be complete without some comment on this aspect of the process. Where it is necessary it can be very important to get it right. Be warned: any omissions in contracts can cost you dear – every detail needs to be got right.

You should thus consider carefully what contractual elements are involved, when they are best introduced and how this should be dealt with to make it acceptable; and to make it stick, especially if anything untoward happens further down the line.

A contract is there for protection. It secures against what might happen if – for whatever reason or circumstance – agreement is not implemented. Sometimes the penalty is considerable; if terms and conditions are not met a significant amount of money may be lost. For example, if you book a wedding reception and then the bride and groom fall out and there is no wedding, there may still be a large bill to pay. The venue owners, perhaps unable to re-let the facility at short notice, invoke the conditions and protect themselves against such loss of revenue.

Acceptable terms

Certain factors are important if any contract is to be acceptable and not seen as inappropriate, draconian or otherwise unsuitable. If you are introducing it, make sure that what you do will:

- Allow no possibility of misunderstandings because everything is clearly communicated.
- Enhance the relationships involved, if necessary on a continuing basis.
- Allow the progressing and securing of agreement to proceed effectively and promptly.
- Allows any necessary flexibility within the arrangement, despite tight terms.
- Link logically and neatly to the practicalities involved.

THE POLICY UNDERLYING CONTRACTS

The first question may be to check who it is that makes policy decisions and with whom you should consult. If you are in charge of such matters, fine; if not you may still have an input to make. Look out for any circumstances not covered by existing policy and be ready to feedback information that may assist with any policy change or update that may be indicated.

Returning to the wedding reception example, the venue operator might decide that stricter terms and conditions, and penalties for cancellation, are necessary on a seasonal basis. A wedding function lost in, say, February is perhaps more damaging than in peak season when it is likely to be easier to find a substitute.

The essentials elements
Contractual arrangements of all sorts need to make clear the:

- Basis of the agreement.
- Terminology to be used by both parties (for instance, is postponing a wedding different from cancellation?).
- Elements of time, dates, and deadlines.
- Procedures, documentation and administration involved.
- Financial details in unambiguous detail.

You need to be thorough: think through the details and make sure they are comprehensively included early on.

WHEN TO INTRODUCE CONTRACTUAL MATTERS
The fact of a contract may cause problems if it also causes surprise. Produce a ten-page document for signature after hours of debate and discussion that contained no mention of the need for it, and people will twitch; and rightly so. You must make matters clear early in the proceedings and, when you introduce it, do:

- Not apologise for the arrangement, though you may need to explain its necessity.
- Emphasise the mutual advantages.
- Use language that stresses the joint benefits of clarity, for example, talk about working together.
- Introduce the contractual side progressively, sufficiently early, and set the scene for any detailed discussion about it that may be necessary later (exactly how to do so may need some planning).
- Check to ensure no detail is missed. Make sure all necessary information is to hand, or secured and recorded if it is to be part of the agreement.

The process is progressive and dealing with it may well be better spread throughout the meeting, rather than as one lengthy aspect of the conversation.

HOW TO DEAL WITH CONTRACTUAL MATTERS

A systematic approach to dealing with contractual matters is therefore likely to be best and creates the greatest likelihood of it ensuring that no problems or objections ensue. While the details of actually drafting the (legal) terms of a contract are beyond our brief here, it is worth noting that this needs some care. It may also need professional legal advice, yet it is advantageous to all if the final document is clear and easy to read; the legal input may be essential, but the tendency to produce text that is, well let's just say off-putting, needs to be watched.

With the core contractual terms considered and documented you can move on to introducing and using this aspect of the matter into negotiations.

A progressive approach

Going through nine stages will give you a proven way to put over all that is necessary:

1. **First mention**: Here careful timing is necessary. The right moment may pass and it will then get ever more difficult to say: "We must have this in writing". Waiting for the other party to raise things may not be best; you have to plan and be prepared to move the conversation onto the matter. A first mention may simply aim to gain agreement on the need for discussion about it. It may also prompt a decision about how and when in the discussion this will be done.

2. **Put details over clearly**: Your communication must be crystal clear. For instance, there can be different interpretations of one word – when does provisional become permanent? Any such confusion may cause disproportionately greater problems later on. This links to what was said about written clarity; it can be difficult to put over key, essentially straightforward, points in a meeting if what you are showing the other party in writing is a convoluted nightmare of jargon.

3. **Emphasise figures and timing for clarity**: It is worth being really pedantic about numbers of all sorts. For example, when, exactly, is the end of the month or year? Again, misunderstanding of such a detail can cause real problems.

4. **Check understanding progressively**: Sometimes this is as simple as just saying, "Is that clear?" occasionally, but it is always very important. Do not just assume matters are clearly understood between you – act so that you are sure.

5. **Document your side of arrangements**: Having made things clear and agreed them, then say how you will confirm it and do just that. Delays can cause confusion. It may also help precision of agreement if you take the initiative – write things down in detail, then they can simply say they agree. Sometimes you may want to do this the other way round to save you time; with a supplier, for example, get them to document the details so that you can agree. But remember to be careful and always read the small print.

6. **Specifically ask for their confirmation**: This will not necessarily come unasked; you need to ask for it. And chase it up if necessary. If contractual arrangements are understood and agreed, you do not have to be circumspect about this, indeed any dilatory behaviour at this stage may be a sign of potential difficulty to come that needs noting as you look ahead.

7. **Follow up to prompt action**: If people ignore some key stage, it is crucial to prompt them and you should not feel awkward about reminding them. Make sure you do not forget, put a note in the diary if matters stretch over some time. Delay might well be in the other party's interest, if not in yours.

8. **Pitch it appropriately**: You need to take a positive approach to contractual matters, stressing that they are important and that they are there to help both parties. Deal with them in a way that appears efficient, professional and which will achieve what you want in a way that doesn't ruffle any feathers.

9. **Look ahead**: An agreement and contract made today set the scene for the future. You may want to begin to touch on future arrangements as you tie down a current one. This can pay dividends over time.

When you need to respond
Sometimes, of course, it will be you receiving the contract. The rules in that case are also straightforward:

- Listen, read and check everything that is put over to you, to make sure you truly understand all the implications.
- Take a moment, in fact as much time as necessary, to consider or to confer with anyone else appropriate (including, on occasion, a legal advisor).
- Be absolutely sure that you can live with the implications, including those of the worst-case scenario, before you add your signature.
- Someone pushing you to sign and conclude matters with undue pressure could be a sign that more thought is necessary and a good reason to consider further.

An important last point here is: never agree to something in haste, or you could well find yourself repenting at leisure – and a bad deal can have long lasting implications.

IF BREAKDOWN OCCURS
When contractual matters are well dealt with there should be minimal problems. But what if something contractual is agreed and then the other party fails to comply in some way? There are few options, you can:

- **Apply the letter of the law**: One way forward is simply to stick to the terms exactly. That is what they are there for. They were agreed. There is no need to feel bad about invoking the conditions. Sometimes this approach will go unchallenged and cause no problems. If not, or if you are yourself worried about souring future arrangements, you may need to seek alternative formulae.

- **Negotiate a compromise**: If you feel so inclined, you can be generous and suggest something less than the full terms. You may make some other arrangement that will foster goodwill without your losing anything significant. If the situation is reversed you may want to insist this is done to minimise any damage inflicted on you (this may necessitate a mini-negotiation within the negotiation; indeed this may a worthwhile digression).
- **Allow an exception**: This is really a variant of the compromise above. In the case of the wedding referred to earlier, a postponement at a time when another booking is easily obtained may guarantee that another venue is not sought for the rescheduled date and introduce considerable goodwill in a business dependent to a large degree on recommendation. Whatever is done, in whatever situation, it may be important to make it clear that it's an exception and sets no precedents for the future. If this point is strongly made it may be felt that you are being very reasonable, and this may lead to return compromise at a later date (something about which it is worth keeping a note).

In such circumstances you need to avoid immediate losses, but balance this with creating advantages of a more long-term nature. Selecting the way forward must incorporate:

- Deciding appropriate policy and introduce contractual matters into any meeting in a way that sets the scene for what you want to do.
- Displaying sensitivity to the details involved and ensuring mutual understanding of the complete package.
- Deploying a systematic approach to the way contractual matters are integrated into the overall conversation.
- Checking – perhaps repeatedly – before anything is signed off.
- Weighing up the advantages/disadvantages in terms of the severity with which you apply the letter of the law.

Whenever detailed contractual arrangements are part of negotiation, care is necessary or confusion can arise all too easily. You are wise always to be circumspect in this area.

There are questions to ask before matters are finalised: what needs including in any policy for contractual matters you may have?; Is all the necessary information available as a prompt for the discussion – a checklist, for example, to ensure you do not miss any tricks?; What level of documentation does your situation demand and does it need origination or review?

You may not always need something in writing, but if careful consideration shows there is even half a chance it might be needed, put matters in writing and make sure that the final statement will do the job you want, securing the details and yet not putting people off you or the agreement, or making them wary either immediately or in the future.

Chapter 9

FOCUSING ON THE KEY ISSUES
Attention to detail

'The fellow that agrees with everything you say is either a fool, or is getting ready to skin you.'
Frank McKinney Hubbard

Negotiation may be well described as part art, part science, and even going about it in the "right way" does not guarantee success, though it might increase the likelihood of it. It needs to be conducted in a way that is well planned, yet flexible, and that recognises that the people element is an important – and the least predictable – one.

Having dissected the process, let us move towards the end by looking at what overall factors add power and certainty to what you do.

ORCHESTRATION IS ESSENTIAL
There is, as we have surely seen, a good deal going on when you negotiate. Undertaking negotiation successfully means you must see the process fully, take a broad view and continue to do so throughout the process; and yes, you also need to worry about the details.

A good grasp of the principles involved will surely help, for it is that which makes everything more manageable and allows you the opportunity to orchestrate and finetune the process as you proceed. Small adjustments as you progress can make all the difference to both how matters proceed and to the outturn. Selecting the mix of tactic that suit what you are trying to do and help you towards your goal must be a considered process; it is one that starts with your planning and also necessitates you being quick on your feet throughout any meeting as you tailor your approach to the particular circumstances of the moment. Something full of complex financial details poses different problems from something simpler.

Dangers to avoid

Beyond careful deployment of positive techniques there are some things to avoid, so *never* allow yourself to:

- Over-react if responses are negative; and remember that the other person is doubtless at pains not to say how excellent every point is.
- Become over-emotional, unpleasant, provocative or insulting; a planned and controlled display of emotion may be useful (on occasion), but you must only do so on a considered basis.
- Agree to something you do not want; in many situations there is a minimal deal which your plan should identify, below which it is better to walk away.

ADDING POWER

Each time you negotiate with someone, and however well or badly it goes, the experience can help build your expertise. It helps you finetune what works well, avoid approaches that work less well, and build on what best fits with your style, and can help in future.

The detail is important. Sometimes what makes the difference between success and failure is small and seemingly insignificant. One phrase, even one gesture, may change things. If all the details are right, the whole will be more likely to work well. So powerful is the possibility of learning from experience and refining your skills as you go that it is worth getting into the habit of making some notes after a meeting: noting what went well and what didn't, and doing so in a way that enables you to better prepare your next meeting.

To illustrate this let me refer to another, rather different, publication. This is a hefty ring binder entitled *The Negotiator's Tactic Bank*.

Published by the quaintly named Big Sur Publishing, it is a compendium of over 200 all-time practical and powerful negotiating tactics. There are a number of sections that take you through every stage of the negotiation process: from "Opening shots" to "Asking the right questions", "Traps and how to avoid them" and "Gaining the upper hand", with each illustrated by a selection of tried and tested approaches. All are set out in a similar format and all are intended to provide a quick checklist style reference for the negotiator doing their homework and planning their strategy. Written by a panel of experts, it makes an excellent companion to any book (like this) reviewing the techniques in more conventional form.

One such tactic from this is reproduced here to illustrate the common style and format involved.

Tactic 185: ESTABLISHING RAPPORT AT A STICKY MOMENT

"... so, let's make fresh start ..."

No negotiation is likely to be entirely plain sailing for you. You can plan (indeed you should). You can proceed carefully, finetuning as you go, but sometimes you hit a crisis. Sometimes it is like when you knock a pile of papers off your desk. Even though you see it coming, you know as you do so that it is too late and then the papers are all over the floor. So, too, with sticky moments in a negotiation meeting; regardless of what has been going on, you are suddenly aware that the agreement is unravelling in your hands, and your carefully planned strategy hits a crisis.

Making the most of a crisis
The cause of the crisis may be either anticipated, that is something you thought might cause problems. Or a total surprise – perhaps something you could never have anticipated. Whatever the cause, let us assume that a bad initial reaction – because you are thrown – makes things worse. What do you do?

In Chinese, the word "crisis" is written as two characters: the first is that for the word "chaos", the second is that for "opportunity" – an interesting thought. The job here is not just to recover and do so without digging the hole deeper, it is to recover and restart, with the initiative.

The way it works
Mark Hunt is doing well. He is setting up an arrangement with a new distributor for South East Asia. He is sitting with them in an outdoor restaurant attached to his hotel in Singapore and, although there has been a good deal of toing and froing, everything seems to be coming together well. He ticks off "initial supply of samples" on his list and is contemplating only a handful more of minor matters, so he is surprised when Brian Lim says: "Shouldn't we get back to finalising a start date? Nothing can proceed without that". Surprised, his reply is rather abrupt: "But I thought we had done that – we instigate everything from the start of next year; surely you don't want to go back into all that?"

His colleague to be is now edgy as well. "We must" , he says, "after all ..." Mark interrupts: "But you agreed," he says, "now you're completely ignoring that fact". He sees from the expression on Brian Lim's face that his abrupt manner and annoyance is being taken as an insult. "You asked for the samples to come a month later", Brian continues, "That takes us up against Chinese New Year which, in case you don't realise, disrupts things here for some ten days".

Mark realises his mistake. Logically the first delay put back the start date and there is obviously no point in launching so close to a major public holiday.

It's my fault
This sticky moment is his own fault (he had simply forgotten how the one change affected another point *and* was showing his ignorance about local conditions). What does he do next?

Well, the need is to restart. In this kind of situation, ploughing on and trying to adjust matters may not be sufficient to instigate the change that is necessary. A new start is often best made by taking a step back, and finding a sure foothold on a solid foundation of understanding and agreement from which to restart.

The "butterfingers" approach
Mark adopts what might be called the "butterfingers" approach. He apologises. He admits his mistake. He reassures. And he makes light of his own error – while labelling it (perhaps more acceptably) as a moment of lost concentration. "Goodness, of course you're absolutely

right. My fault; how could I possibly forget that changing the sample delivery date will inevitably delay the launch date. I'm sorry, I thought I was over the jetlag! And I had no intention of suggesting that you were neglecting our agreement. Now, we have agreed so much – it's going to be a great opportunity for us both, I'm sure, but it is complicated. Let me recap just a little; then, as you say, let's get a launch date that's right for us both absolutely clear before we move on".

He can now proceed and no damage should be done to either the relationship or the agreements. Of course, sticky moments can occur for all sorts of reasons, and that fault may lie with you, the other person or just with circumstances. So, you do not always need to start with an apology as Mark did here, but if not a similar restart makes good sense.

CHECKLIST FOR GETTING IT RIGHT

- Do not plough on and risk digging the hole deeper
- Flag that a restart is necessary
- Apologise for any mistake on your part, if necessary
- Mention good things (linked perhaps to the stage that has been reached)
- Move forward again from an agreed firm foundation, leaving the "stickiness" on one side.

This example is not too long, but may be more than you would want to write as a note following one of your own meetings. Nevertheless the idea of having a standard format to make such notes is a good one, and certainly regular activity in reviewing what you do, what works and noting it to assist planning for future negotiating encounters, is likely to be beneficial; a good habit to get into, perhaps.

Because negotiation is a dynamic, interactive process and one individually deployed, even the best performance can be made more effective. The key things are to start and ensure that the experience you gain makes what you do in future better and better.

As an analogy, remember when you learnt to drive? Driving is a good example here: if you are like me then for a while you probably despaired of ever being able to concentrate on the disparate, long, seemingly endless list of things to think about and do all at once, and that were necessary to make it work. The same thought applies to negotiation. A basic shopping list of techniques will start you off and allow you to practise. Then with the basic techniques in mind you can add to your method of approach and continue to develop it.

A good coach, teaching, say, tennis or golf, will always operate this way; whatever your faults and however many there may be, they will get you to work on them in a manageable way, probably one at a time. The principle is sound. Such conscious use of experience in the light of your awareness and knowledge of the process is the only way to develop real clout. You cannot expect that to come overnight, or without practise and consideration.

AN EYE ON THE FUTURE

Your success (or otherwise) at your next negotiating session will depend as much as anything on you. This book has set out to act as a spur to your abilities, but it is what you do now that matters. What you are able to do depends very much on how consciously you set about it. You need to understand and deploy the techniques appropriately. You also need confidence in your ability to do so effectively. At this point we are, I hope, agreed that you can be a better negotiator if you work at it. Indeed, the process of trying will itself help you learn quicker and do better. Continue this process for a while and you will be a match for anyone.

Resolutions to give you an edge

Let us take stock: it has been repeatedly said that negotiation is a complex process. Complex in that there are many factors to bear in mind rather than that those factors are individually intellectually taxing. You need to understand and deploy a range of techniques. Further, much of what makes it successful is in the details and in the sensitivity with which the process is approached and orchestrated.

So, now as we move towards the end, and in part in a bid to persuade you that it is a manageable process, we focus on ten key areas, some of them leading inevitably to others, which while not together forming a panacea or being entirely comprehensive, help highlight key issues and summarise something of the nature of the process and its tactics. Because of the jargon involved with the negotiation process, there is then a Glossary of the main terms, both to recap and to link to any further review you may undertake.

The first point of the ten is not only important but there is logic in letting it start the list.

1. Preparation

With a process, with the complexity of negotiation, it is not surprising that preparation provides a key foundation to the process. Early on it accelerates the value of experience, and beyond that it acts to create a valuable foundation to the actual negotiation that follows. In one sense, preparation is no more than respect for the old premise that it is best to open your mind before you open your mouth.

Thus, preparation may consist of a few quiet minutes just before you step into a meeting. Alternatively it may consist of sitting down for a couple of hours with colleagues to thrash out the best tactics to adopt; and everything in between. It can be stretched to include rehearsal, a meeting to actually run through what you want to happen, rather as you would rehearse an important presentation. So:

- **Give preparation adequate time** (and in a hectic life that also means starting far enough in advance).
- **Involve the right people** (because they will be involved in the meeting, or just because they can help).
- **Assemble and analyse the necessary information** (and take key facts to the meeting).

Preparation should not assume you can ensure that everything will proceed exactly as planned – planning is as much to help finetune what is being done when circumstances do take an unforeseen turn. Experience may reduce the time preparation takes; it does not however negate it. Remember too the saying attributed to many a famous golfer: "The more that I practice my game, the more good luck I seem to have." Never reject preparation as unnecessary; never skimp it in terms of time and effort. It is too late when you come out of a meeting that has not gone well to say – "If only I had ..."

2. Making your profile contribute

This may seem obvious now but it can have a considerable effect on the outcome of negotiating. A sensible view of the literal aspect of this is clearly prudent – you need to be "smartly turned out" and that needs to be interpreted in light of the circumstances. For example, for a man it might mean a business suit in many contexts, something less formal on occasion and a shirt and tie in a country with a hot climate. Women have more choices to make but the principles to apply are similar.

More important is that certain details give specific impressions, for instance, if you are seen as:

- **Well prepared**, then people give what you say greater weight.
- **Well organised**, has a similar effect.
- **Confident**, this can have a major impact on the credibility of what you say, especially the belief in your insistence that you can do no more.
- **Professional**, again a whole raft of characteristics may contribute to this from being experienced, expert or approachable to something like just appearing not to be rushed; and again the case you make will engender more consideration if the person making it is seen in the right light.

The point here is that something can be done to make any such characteristic more visible where this might help, and sometimes this might become a useful exaggeration. Of course what is said is important, but much judgement comes from visual signals and it is wise therefore to use them.

3. Communicating clearly

Like preparation, the best way to describe this is as a foundation to success. Your communications within a complex negotiation situation need to be absolutely clear. There is a power that flows directly from sheer clarity and good description, people:

- **Understand**: this speaks for itself, but it also means

misunderstandings are avoided and it helps ensure that the meeting stays tightly focused on its real agenda.
- Are **impressed**: clarity gives favourable impressions of authority, certainty and confidence – all of which add to the power you bring to the table. Indeed people are especially impressed when they expect something to be complicated and someone guides them through easily. Clear communication really can score you points.

In addition, clarity about the meeting itself – setting a clear agenda and so on – will direct the proceedings and help make it possible for you to take the lead, which in turn helps get you where you want to go.

Clarity stems from preparation, clear thinking and analysis – and from experience. It is worth working at. The last thing you want at the end of the day is to achieve agreement, only to find it retracted later because someone says that they were not clear what it was they were agreeing to. Insisting at that stage can mean you are never trusted again; it is a position to avoid.

4. Respect the people

Negotiation is a cut and thrust process. It *has* an adversarial aspect to it and everyone involved is very much aware of this. While it may be important to take a tough line, to be firm and to insist, this is always more acceptable if the overall tenure of a meeting is kept essentially courteous.

Show that you understand other peoples' point of view. Be seen to find out what it is, to note details that are important to them and to refer to this during the meeting. Be prepared to apologise, to flatter, to ask opinion and to show respect (in some cases perhaps, whether you feel it is deserved or not!).

Apart from wanting to maintain normal courtesies in what can sometimes be a difficult situation, showing respect can help your case. If you have to take a strong line there is a danger that it can be seen simply as an unreasonable attack; as such the automatic response is a rebuff. If the strong line comes from someone who is clearly expressing respect for others and their views, then it is more likely to be taken seriously, considered and perhaps agreed.

5. Aim High

No apology for returning to this factor; it is undoubtedly one of the most important. Indeed, it conditions much about your whole approach. Aim high. Start by considering, in your planning, what this means. Think about what might be possible, think about what would really be best for you – and go for that. Remember that there are doubtless a list of variables with which to deal – perhaps a long list – and that what you hope to agree is a mix of them all. Consider what is the best overall position – and go for that.

Negotiation is about to and fro debate and about compromise, but it is very easy for compromise to become a foregone conclusion. You can always trade down from an initial stance, but it is very difficult to trade up. Once a meeting is underway and your starting point is on the table, you cannot offer another starting point.

Starting as you mean to go on is an inherent part of aiming high.

6. Get their shopping list

This rule links to the fact that you need to negotiate a package. If you agree parts of a deal individually, you reduce your ability to vary the package because more and more elements of it are fixed. Something may seem straightforward in isolation. You are happy to agree it, yet suddenly you come to other points that you want to negotiate about, and there is nothing left with which to trade.

The principle here is simple. You need to find out the full list of what the other party needs to agree. Then you must not allow parts, possibly important parts, to be picked off and secured one at a time, as a preliminary to hitting you with major demands at a stage where your options are limited.

7. Always keep searching for variables

Variables can be listed as part of your preparation; listed and prioritised. Even a thorough job at that stage can leave things out. *Everything* is negotiable, *everything* is potentially a variable – and this includes things that have specifically been excluded by one party or the other. You may have said something is unchangeable and then decide that you need the power that shifting a little would give you.

Certainly you need to question what the other party means. Does, "That's it, I definitely cannot go any further on this", mean what it says, or only that they hope they will not need to negotiate further about something? Questions, or a challenge, may be necessary to find out. The search for possible variables and different mixes in their respective priority must continue throughout the whole process. As the process demands more compromise from someone, they may have to accept that things they hoped could be regarded as fixed will have to be regarded as variables. And that some variables may need to be more variable than was the original intention

Keep any open-mind, keep searching and assume everything is always a potential variable.

8. Utilise the techniques

Your success in negotiations is less likely to come from some clever ploy or one display of power. It comes through the interlocking details. There is a good deal to keep in mind during a negotiation, and the situation becomes more complicated as negotiations proceed. You can influence matters in a 100 different ways, but they need to be appropriate ways.

The good negotiator deploys a range of techniques, so they need to be familiar with them and able to make the best use of them. But it is not a question of blasting the other party with a hail of techniques; they need using with surgical precision. Just when is it appropriate to be silent or to show unequivocally that you are adamant?

Negotiation must never be allowed to take place on "automatic pilot". Every move must be considered, and this applies as much to *how* you do things as to what you do. Techniques must be made to work for you and the way to do this is on a case-by-case basis – one that reflects what is right for that person, that meeting and that moment of that meeting.

9. Orchestrate: managing and controlling the process

Certainly, overall orchestration is a major issue. It is all too easy to find that the concentration that is necessary to deal with the immediate situation can result in your taking you eye off the ball in terms of the total game plan.

You need to take every possible action to help yourself stand back and work with the full picture. For example:

- Make notes.
- Summarise regularly to recap (and *always* if you feel yourself getting lost; though you do not need to say why).
- Keep as much of an eye on the broad picture as on the needs of the moment.
- Keep your objectives and the desired outcome clearly in mind.
- Be prepared to take whatever action is necessary to keep on top of the situation (e.g. to pause and take stock) despite how you think it may look (in fact such action almost always simply increases the level of confidence you project).

If you approach this aspect of the process consciously, note what helps you, and allow positive habits to become established, then your experience and competence will build positively and quickly.

10. Never lower your guard

Never relax for a single second. Even when things are going well, when events seem to be following your plan accurately, when one agreement is following another – be wary. Do not relax your attempts to read between the lines in such circumstances and do not assume that the positive path will continue. If you assume anything at all, assume that there is danger, reversal or surprise just round the corner and be ready for it.

Remember that *both* parties are doing their best to meet their own objectives and that the other person is just as likely to be playing a long game as to be a pushover. It is not over until it is over, and it is often late in the day that things come out of the woodwork and change what looked like, until that moment, a straightforward agreement.

Finally under this last heading, remember the words, quoted earlier and accredited to Lord Hore-Belisha: "When a man tells me he is going to put all his cards on the table, I always look up his sleeve". It is good advice.

As was said, by focusing on the ten points above it is not intended to devalue anything else, and it should always be remember that successful negotiation is a matter of getting many details right together. The first step to making it work is to understand the principles and something of the techniques and how to deploy them. With that in mind you need a conscious approach so that you make your experience build fast and note what works well for you to strengthen your negotiating ability in the future.

PERSONAL CHARACTERISTICS
What does all this mean in terms of you and the characteristics you must cultivate to be a good negotiator? A final ten point list summarises those characteristics:

1. Know how to read and assess their opponents (in terms of their needs, plans etc.).
2. Know how to assess the strengths and weaknesses the first assessment implies (and also which people in a team are key players and in what role).
3. Know how to maximise and minimise aspects of the case as appropriate.
4. Be a master at timing, judging accurately when to reveal, or not, their views.
5. Confident in using silence and prompting the other person to say, and reveal, more.
6. Have a straight face and an ability to bluff.
7. Be able to use the threat of breakdown effectively (and not to overuse it).
8. Know how to distract, back off or put the pressure on when appropriate.
9. Be effective at applying psychological pressure.
10. Constantly question their opponent's position, especially when under threat.

You may assess your abilities higher in some areas than others, but all of these are areas on which you can build and do so progressively. All are affected positively by confidence and with the knowledge you now have after reviewing the whole process in some detail, your confidence should be growing. All that remains is to put it into practice – you just need to give it go.

FINALLY:
On a lighter note ...

For all the need to take negotiation seriously if you are to be successful at it, it is also in some ways a funny old business – so let's end with the old story of the very first negotiation in history; it's a story that shows it needs to be got right.

In the Garden of Eden Adam is comfortable, but lonely. He calls out to God telling him how he feels and God's voice replies from the heavens: "I have the perfect solution, I can create woman for you". Adam is pleased to hear there is a solution, but asks: "What's a woman, Lord?"

"Woman will be my greatest creation", says God, "She will be intelligent, caring, sensitive, and her beauty will surpass anything on Earth. She will understand your every mood, care for you in every way, and she will make you happier than you can imagine. She will be the perfect partner for you. But there will be cost". "She certainly sounds wonderful" said Adam, "but what will the cost be exactly?" "Well," said God "Let's say an arm, three fingers and your right ear".

Despite the promised return, Adam is not very happy about this. He ponders the arrangement for some time, finally saying, "I think that's really too much to ask – what would I get for, say, just one rib?"

And the rest, as they say, is history; though I should say here that I have met as many women who are good negotiators as I have men – maybe more. But this lighter example certainly shows that variances in terms and conditions can radically change the outcome of any negotiation. Well-executed negotiation is an essential tool in getting the deal you want.

Glossary

There are certainly a number of technical terms stemming from the negotiating process. Some of these are worth noting and have a precise meaning, which is important to the successful practice of negotiation.

Arbitration
This term is usually applied to negotiation designed to settle disputes, especially where negotiations involve a third-party and both sides agree to be bound by their, objective, decisions. In the United Kingdom, ACAS – The Advisory Conciliation and Arbitration Service – is a national body able to provide help when organisations fall out).

Bargaining
Another word implying negotiation (one which has fewer business connotations and makes the process sound simpler); essentially it is a euphemism for negotiation, albeit one that implies the least complex end of the scale.

Blocking
A blocking statement is one designed to stop argument and channel discussions in a particular direction; it is a prefix to the point being made.

Body language
The signs given out through someone's stance, behaviour and gestures which (with varying degrees of accuracy) can cast some light on the status of a conversation – or in this case negotiation.

Bogeys
Factors used with the express purpose of adding weight to what is being

said; may or may not be of real significance.

Bridge of rapport
Factors introduced to make discussion easier, to prompt discussion and openness and which also direct the conversation along the right lines, i.e. one that will help whoever is introducing the bridge.

Collective Agreements (and Bargaining)
A term implying that the agreements made, and thus the negotiation however many people are involved in it, is on behalf of a larger group and that all those in the group will be bound by the agreement made.

Concession
A variable that is conceded as part of the trading process; concessions can vary in significance and may be made to appear more or less significant as such helps the case.

Contract
A contract is a legally binding agreement which is often one of the end results of a negotiation.

Deadlock
A stage at which no progress towards agreement is being made, but from which progress is still potentially possible (as opposed to stalemate, which is a breakdown without any agreement being made).

Defend/attack spiral
A progressive attack, each stage of which will be resisted and which by definition gives warning of negative responses to come.

Escalation
A technique that involves going back on previous offers and asking for more at a stage where someone's position of power has improved and agreement can likely be forced.

Fall-back position
This is essentially "Plan B". When aiming as high as you wish will

manifestly not work, you may need to settle for something less – the fall-back position defines the starting point for this.

Icebergs
This, as the name implies, indicates something largely hidden. In this case, it is the reasons why something is rejected. A superficial reason may be the sign of underlying and more fundamental factors of disagreement that need to be got out into the open.

Irritators
Words or phrases that add nothing to the negotiator's persuasiveness and are likely to be taken in exactly the opposite way from that stated. Thus saying, "This is fair and reasonable", just alerts people to the fact that it almost certainly is not, at least as far as they are concerned.

Legitimacy
This term classifies factual evidence used to support a case – it must not just seem factual; it must be largely unarguable to warrant the term.

Loss leader
A variable that someone finds unimportant and is prepared to sacrifice (ideally in return for something better); its importance will, nevertheless, be maximised to help make an effective trade.

Must-haves
The reverse of the loss-leader; factors that are so important that nothing, or nothing significant, can be given away. A true must-have may well mean that no deal is better than the wrong one.

Neutrality
Operating from a neutral position, not putting all your cards on the table at once and apparently remaining open to a variety of solutions.

Nibbling
The technique of posing last minute additional requests at a stage where it is judged that agreement will come rather than risk the total deal that is so nearly secured.

Ploy
A tactical move in negotiation usually designed to act negatively and stop something, rather than promote a positive move; hence "spoiling tactics".

Point of balance
The place at the end of all the toing and froing where agreement is possible and a package of terms and conditions is acceptable to both parties.

Positional bargaining
The opposite of the win-win approach, when both parties push their case in isolation of the other and the likelihood is an entrenched position or, if there is an agreement, then one party is left feeling seriously aggrieved.

Power
Many of the approaches used in negotiation produce power; in other words, they make the case being made have more "weight" and be less likely to be resisted.

Precedent
Using examples of past success to demonstrate the potential or likely success of something similar being discussed currently.

Psychological attack
Tactics designed purely to rattle or unnerve someone; usually in themselves of no great import, but made effective because of good timing and the confidence with which they are deployed.

Quick kill
A take-it-or-leave-it approach designed to end negotiations almost before they have begun; risks major breakdown when used at an early stage.

Signposting
A general communications term for increasing clarity and understanding by flagging in advance where a line of conversation is

going; it can apply to either the content or the nature of what is being said.

Soviet-style negotiation
A "win at all costs" approach; can easily prove self-defeating.

Stalemate
An irretrievable breakdown of negotiations with no possibility of further progress; as opposed to a deadlock which might potentially be broken.

Stance
The point from which a negotiator is operating at any particular moment; hence "initial stance" (the position taken up at the start of a meeting).

Trading
The concept of not giving variables away, but trading or exchanging them in some way (with this goes the idea of maximising the weight of those given, and minimising the worth of those accepted).

Threat of punishment
Apparent or actual refusal to agree to some specific element important to the other party, especially where this can be done from a position of power and the (seeming) ability to make it stick.

Variable
The elements – or individual terms and conditions – that negotiation aims to arrange and agree a basis for; these are the basis of the concept of trading and of making, or winning, concessions.

Zone of agreement
The range within which an agreement is possible; an initial stance may be outside this, but final discussions must settle in this bargaining range (this concept was originated by Howard Raffa in *The Art and Science of Negotiation* [Bellnap Press at Harvard University]).

www.ingramcontent.com/pod-product-compliance
Lightning Source LLC
Chambersburg PA
CBHW022155080426
42734CB00006B/438